Letters to the Early Church

A Devotional Commentary on Ephesians through Thessalonians

LETTERS TO THE EARLY CHURCH

A Devotional Commentary on Ephesians through Thessalonians

GENERAL EDITOR

Leo Zanchettin

The Word Among Us Press
9639 Doctor Perry Road
Ijamsville, Maryland 21754
www.wordamongus.org
ISBN: 1-59325-037-1

08 07 06 05 04 1 2 3 4 5 6
ISBN: 1-59325-037-1

Cover design by David Crosson

Made and printed in the United States of America.

Library of Congress Control Number: 2004105259

Table of Contents

Acknowledgments

We want to thank everyone who has made this commentary possible, especially all of the writers who contributed meditations. Some of the meditations appearing in this book were initially developed for *The Word Among Us* monthly publication, and we are grateful to these writers for granting us permission to reprint their work. We also want to thank Fr. Joseph Mindling, O.F.M. Cap., Fr. Joseph Wimmer, O.S.A., Fr. George Montague, S.M., and Mrs. Jody Vaccaro Lewis, Ph.D., for contributing the introductory chapters, as well as Bob French for his chapter on Paul's prison experience. A special note of thanks also goes to Jeanne Kun and Hallie Riedel for their considerable contributions to the meditations. And finally, we want to thank Kathy Mayne for her tireless administrative work in gathering all the material that went into this book. May the Lord abundantly bless each of them!

Leo Zanchettin

Introduction

Fifteen years ago, I was twenty-seven years old, single, living in Maryland, and contemplating a life of celibacy for the sake of the kingdom of God. Today, I'm married, live in Florida, and have three children. Many things I expected to happen in my life did not happen, and a number of unexpected occurrences did happen—all resulting in the happiness I now know as a husband, father, and Catholic editor.

If fifteen years can bring so much change to one life, imagine what fifteen years can do in the life of a whole group of people. Imagine how different any group—a family, a company, a social club, or even a church—would look that many years after it was first formed. Well, that's one of the greatest benefits of a book like this one. By looking at the letters that have been collected in this commentary, we can get a glimpse into the way the early church developed. Beginning with 1 Thessalonians, which Paul wrote around A.D. 50, and ending with Ephesians, which dates near the end of Paul's life in the mid-sixties, we see a church growing, not only in numbers but more importantly in revelation and understanding of its role in the world.

In A.D. 50, many Christians hoped and thought that Jesus was coming back very soon. All eyes were on heaven, waiting for him to appear and take all who had been faithful to him into his eternal kingdom. Since the Second Coming was imminent, the believers' main concerns had to do with keeping themselves pure and blameless so they could be with the Lord (1 Thessalonians 1:9-10). Separation from the world was key, as they sought to live quietly and mind their own affairs. After all, they were waiting for judgment day, which would come "like a thief in the night" (4:10-12; 5:2).

But Jesus didn't come back, and time kept marching on. And as it did, the Christians faced new challenges. Not only were they called to keep themselves pure and free from sin, they also had to hold fast to the gospel in a world filled with competing philosophies and religions (Colossians 2:8,20-23). They had to learn how to establish and maintain close relationships with one another—relationships based not just on a mutual eagerness for the Second Coming but on a common mind and a shared desire to become more like Christ (Philippians 2:1-5; 4:2-3). And finally, they had to learn that God didn't just want to bring them to heaven as soon as possible, but to bind them together in a love and a unity so strong that it would be a visible revelation of his own divine mind (Ephesians 3:9).

This little lesson in early church development has more to teach us than a few points of history. In a way, each of us experiences in our own life a parallel kind of development as we grow in faith. When we first come to know the Lord in a personal way, a longing for heaven is sparked in us that makes us want nothing more than to be with him. Over time, however, as our relationship with the Lord deepens, we come to understand that God has called us for a purpose, and that this purpose has to do with being his witnesses in this world. We still long for heaven, but we also know that we have already been raised with Christ (Colossians 3:1) and are now invited to join him in the task of advancing the kingdom by fulfilling the "good works" that God has in store for us (Ephesians 2:10). And so, with our hearts fixed on Jesus, we are happy to walk in this world as his ambassadors, manifesting his love, power, and mercy to everyone around us.

It was with these thoughts in mind that we put together this commentary on the Letters to the Ephesians, Philippians, Colossians, and Thessalonians. Each of the meditations in this book speaks in a different way about God's desire to help us mature in Christ and about how we can best respond to his invitation to a deeper life with him. They give us a vision of the kind of transformation that can happen over time as we let the Holy Spirit teach us how to translate our initial enthusiasm into a permanent, life-giving commitment to the Lord. Just as the church grew and matured, and even changed over time, so can we. All we need is to keep close to Jesus, immerse ourselves in Scripture, and try every day to stay in step with the Holy Spirit. If we do, who knows what our lives will look like in fifteen years?

Leo Zanchettin
General Editor

Unlocking Paul's Chains
The Story behind Paul's Prison Letters

by Bob French

A painting by Rembrandt depicts the apostle Paul seated on a bed in a gloomy prison cell with a faint light shining through the bars. Next to him is a sword, which Rembrandt used to symbolize Scripture as the "sword of the Spirit" (Ephesians 6:17). As he holds a pen and a manuscript, presumably one of his letters, Paul's eyes reveal deep suffering but also communicate his firm intent to spread the gospel.

Trying to uncover the history behind Paul's prison letters is somewhat like looking at this painting: It is very hard to get a completely factual picture with what we are given. Nevertheless, what we can see shows us pretty much what we need to see. The historical details are scarce, and sometimes they are not there at all. Sometimes all we have to work with are the Scriptures themselves, but all the evidence still leaves us with the same impression—that God's hand was just as much at work in Paul's life as in his letters, transforming it into a vehicle for the good news.

Filling in the Background. Admittedly, we don't know exactly which letters Paul wrote from prison. Many believe that Ephesians, Philippians, and Colossians were prison letters. As for when and where, the debate also continues—between two "majority opinions." One claims that he wrote all of them during his first imprisonment in Rome (about A.D. 60), and another holds that he wrote them earlier, either at Ephesus, in Greece, or Caesarea, in Judea. The most probable location seems to be Ephesus, because Paul often talks about sending people to the churches he is writing to, which would be much easier if he were writing from a location in Greece than from one in Rome or Palestine.

But figuring out the "which," the "where," and the "when" of Paul's letters isn't so much important as understanding the "why," the "what," and the "how." Why was Paul in prison? What happened there, and how did this experience affect the letters? And of course, what can all of this teach us?

The most complete record of Paul's life, the Book of Acts, tells us that Paul was imprisoned for a variety of reasons. In Philippi, he and Silas were accused by Romans of being Jews who were disrupting a legitimate business (fortunetelling), and advocating practices that went against Roman customs (Acts 16:16-21). In Ephesus, the Greeks said that he was ruining their trade in silver shrines by saying that man-made gods are no gods at all (19:26). In Caesarea and Jerusalem, groups of Jews accused him of deliberately stirring up their people and being part of the "Nazarene sect" (chapters 21-26). As most of these examples show, his accusers generally viewed Paul as little more than a troublemaker.

Paul's response to these accusations shows us the real reason for his imprisonment: God was using it for his purposes. In his speech to King Agrippa, Paul makes it clear that he is being sent to his own people and to the Gentiles, to "open their eyes" (Acts 26:17-18). In fact, the Romans couldn't find any reason why Paul should be imprisoned, let alone killed. According to King Agrippa, Paul could have been set free and avoided Roman imprisonment had he not appealed his case to Caesar (26:32). But Paul saw things in a different light altogether: Near the end of Acts, he tells the Jews of Rome why he is confined: "It is for the sake of the hope of Israel that I am bound with these chains" (28:20).

Rods and Chains. The exact conditions of Paul's prison life are hard to pin down, since we have no record of them. But the evidence of Scripture, combined with what we know about the prisons of the time, can show us what he might have experienced.

Acts tells us that one of Paul's worst imprisonments was his first, at Philippi. The description given there jibes with history very closely. The prisoners were severely flogged, probably with rods, which although a lesser punishment than scourging, still caused bloody wounds. (Paul knew this punishment well, for in 2 Corinthians he writes that he received it three times at the hands of his Jewish brothers—2 Corinthians 11:25.)

After being beaten, the prisoners were thrown into the prison's "inner room" and put in stocks. The Romans often reserved such rooms for the lowest class of inmates. Like the *Tullianum*, an underground cell in Rome's Mamartine Prison, where Paul may have awaited execution, they were often dark, damp, cold, and usually overcrowded. The stocks used in those days were extremely painful, since they prevented the prisoner from moving or sleeping. Paul was fortunate that he stayed there only a few days.

With the exception of his imprisonment at Philippi and his last stay in Rome, Paul's other prison experiences were most likely not as harsh, although still quite unpleasant. From Paul's frequent references to chains, we can guess that during most of his time in prison he was chained to one or more guards with manacles on his hands. These manacles were often heavy, weighing at least ten pounds, and could be quite painful. Paul apparently lived under this form of military custody during his first stay in Rome while he was under house arrest, living in his own rented apartment and awaiting trial (Acts 28:16). He may not have been chained all the time, but possibly had some freedom of movement, at least during the day.

An Opportunity for Ministry. Besides the fact that he was in chains, there are many things we can tell about Paul's prison life from his own letters. Obviously, he must have had the freedom to write. It is beyond question that many other prisoners of the time were able to write; anecdotes show philosophers, poets, and playwrights engaged in their work, so surely Paul must have been able to compose letters.

We can also say that Paul must have been allowed visitors. The very fact that he wrote letters in prison means that someone must have carried them out for him, and that someone must have given him materials to write with. Prisoners could and often did receive material goods as well. Paul mentions one such visitor in Philippians, for example; he thanks the Philippians for the gift he has received "from Epaphroditus" (4:18).

While it was certainly not unheard of for prisoners of that era to receive visits from friends and relatives, it could be very dangerous, since the visitors often risked being thrown in prison themselves. But as one scholar points out, the early Christians were especially conscious of the duty to visit the imprisoned, since so many of them were being persecuted and since Jesus had specifically mentioned prisons in his teaching: "I was in prison and you visited me" (Matthew 25:36).

Perhaps the most interesting aspect of Paul's time in prison was that it was an opportunity for ministry, both inside and outside his place of confinement. The most famous example is the story of the Philippian jailer who received the gospel from Paul after an earthquake (Acts 16:29-34). But Scripture scholars have noted other examples. For instance, after Paul is imprisoned in Caesarea, the governor Felix has several meetings with him, which could well have included evangelism (24:26). Then, when Paul goes to Rome, he spends an entire day preaching the gospel to the Jews while under house arrest (28:23).

That Paul should find strength to preach in prison is no surprise, considering the numerous examples of Christian prisoners throughout history who converted others through their witness. For example, we know that in St. Maximilian Kolbe's starvation bunker, the dying prisoners could be heard praying and singing hymns to the Lord.

What is perhaps more amazing is how Paul reached so many in the outside world while still in prison. The letters, of course, are proof of that, since they have been touching people with the gospel ever since the first churches received them centuries ago. But Paul also sent out disciples from prison to build up the churches. He tells the Ephesians that he is sending Tychicus, his "dear brother and a faithful minister," to encourage them (Ephesians 6:21). In Philemon, he mentions that he is sending Onesimus, who has become his "child" while in prison (Philemon 10).

An Ambassador in Chains. One commentator has claimed that Paul's imprisonment had very little impact on these letters. But that's almost like saying that applesauce is not made of apples! On the contrary, the letters themselves show us that Paul's imprisonment had a great deal to do with how he saw himself and his mission, and how he communicated it to the church.

In Ephesians, Paul describes himself as "a prisoner for Christ Jesus for the sake of you Gentiles" (3:1). Perhaps this is one reason why Paul does not give many details about his imprisonment: He is too focused on his goal to give us the "tape recorder and camera" description we might like.

Two more times in Ephesians, Paul specifically mentions his circumstances, but only in relation to Christ. He again calls himself a "prisoner in the Lord" (4:1) and later, an "ambassador in chains" (6:20). The image of an ambassador would have been a memorable one for his readers, as Roman ambassadors were very powerful people who were chosen above all for their loyalty. But an ambassador "in chains" was even more radical.

Paul wanted his readers to understand that his chains were not as binding as they might think. In fact, they were doing the work of evangelization! In the opening lines of Philippians, he declares, "I want you to know, beloved, that what has happened to me has actually helped to spread the gospel" (1:12). How can that be? Because his imprisonment has motivated other Christians to proclaim the word of God courageously (1:14).

Certainly by speaking of his chains, Paul was also trying to encourage the Philippians. He was definitely concerned with how they viewed his situation. By assuring them that his chains "really" advanced the gospel, scholars claim, Paul may have been thinking of the shame that was attached to being a prisoner. There is no doubt that the ancient world held prisoners in very low esteem, and Paul's words of bravery and commitment to Jesus would have gone a long way in taking away any sense of embarrassment his followers may have felt for him.

While trying to encourage the churches that he was not in a hopeless situation, Paul also wanted encouragement himself. We can see this concern in all three letters—and each time it is associated again with Paul's chains. In Philippians 1:20-21, Paul expresses hope that he will not be "put to shame" but will continue to exalt Christ, whether in life or in death. In both Ephesians and Colossians, after talking of his chains, Paul asks for prayers that he might declare the gospel "boldly" and "clearly" (Ephesians 6:20; Colossians 4:4).

God's Hand at Work. The fact that Paul spent so much time in prison is crucially important to the way we understand both him and his letters. Through all of it, we can see God's hand at work: in allowing Paul the freedom to write; in giving him visitors to carry his letters to the world; and perhaps most importantly, in allowing him to suffer what he did. God was able to work through Paul, perhaps even more effectively, because his suffering served to bring others to Christ. These letters beg the question: How would the churches have developed if Paul had never been imprisoned for the sake of Christ? If Paul had not undergone these trials, would believers today still be encouraged by his words?

There is one other thing Paul's prison experience shows us: He was not a "lone ranger." The reason Paul was able to carry out his ministry under such difficult circumstances is that through his letters, he reached out to a community of believers, of which he was only one member. Paul consistently encouraged his brothers and sisters, even by name, thanked them for supporting him, and asked for their prayers. And perhaps most importantly, he knew he was never alone. He kept a joyful heart, following his own advice in Ephesians: "Sing and make melody to the Lord in your hearts, giving thanks to God the Father at all times for everything in the name of our Lord Jesus Christ" (5:19-20).

Unity and Love in Christ

The Letter to the Ephesians

An Introduction to the Letter to the Ephesians

by Jody Vaccaro Lewis, Ph.D.

The Letter to the Ephesians represents one of St. Paul's most beautiful meditations on the nature of the church and what it means to be a Christian based on unity and love in Christ. Here we have a powerful message about how we are all called by the grace of God, saved through the redemption of Christ, and empowered by the Holy Spirit to live in peace and unity as members of the body of Christ. This message is one that, as St. Thomas Aquinas commented, strengthens our faith through encouragement and reassurance, blessings and praise.

While the letter is timeless in its appeal, Paul was originally writing to Christians in a different historical place and time than ours, so it makes sense to begin with a brief look at the original audience and date of the letter. Then we can focus on the themes of the letter and how they continue to speak to us today.

Where Did This Letter Come From? Unlike many of his other letters, Paul does not give specific details about the audience of this letter, such as names of individuals or specific circumstances. This is rather surprising, since we know that Paul spent more than two years in Ephesus (Acts 19) and would have known that community very well. Scholars also point out that the address to those "in Ephesus" (Ephesians 1:1) is absent from the oldest manuscripts of the letter. Since it does not address a particular situation or problem, unlike Paul's other letters, many scholars think that the letter was intended as a circular letter to be read by one community, perhaps beginning with Ephesus, and then passed on to the next. Otherwise, it's possible that Paul simply decided to write a more general letter to the Ephesians.

Who were the Ephesians, and what was Ephesus like? Ephesus was an important ancient city on the western coast of Asia Minor (in the country we call Turkey today). It was a good choice for Paul's missionary work, since it was relatively near other cities such as Thessalonica, Corinth, and Philippi. It was a wealthy, flourishing city and home to the largest Greek temple in the ancient world, along with other impressive buildings. The population of Ephesus has been estimated at 250,000, and it was peopled by Greeks, Romans, and Jews alike. With all of these groups, there were many different religions and cults, and Paul had his work cut out for him. However, he had some helpers in Priscilla and Aquila, a Christian wife and husband who began evangelizing there in the early 50s A.D. while Paul traveled to other communities. He then returned for his long and successful stay in Ephesus (Acts 18:19–19:41), spreading the gospel across the region.

As for the date of the letter, Paul mentions being an "ambassador in chains" (Ephesians 6:20), which suggests that he was in prison. Although Paul was jailed on more than one occasion for preaching the gospel, the reference in this letter is probably to Paul's imprisonment in Rome in the early 60s A.D., sometime before his death. Maybe he was moved during this experience to meditate on the themes of unity and love to one of his favorite communities. However, if Paul were not writing exclusively to the Ephesians, it would make sense at this time for him to write a more general letter of praise and encouragement that could be circulated among his communities even if he were not among them.

Finally, we need to acknowledge that many scholars are uncertain as to whether Paul actually wrote Ephesians himself. We know that during Paul's time, an author would sometimes write in the name of another person who was the original source of the main ideas or teaching. In other words, the author did not want to plagiarize but to give credit where credit was due. If we compare Ephesians with other letters of Paul, such as Romans, we may see certain differences regarding linguistic and stylistic elements, historical elements that may suggest a later period in the church, and theological elements that may indicate a further development of thought. If the letter reflects many such differences, it may be classified as pseudonymous (meaning that it is written in someone else's name).

So, if Paul did not write the letter himself, he may have delegated a coworker to write it in his name, or it may have been written by one of his followers after his death as a way of preserving his teachings. In this sense, we must note, the author of the letter should still be thought of and referred to as Paul, since the letter is part of the Pauline tradition. That is also why these letters were included in the New Testament and are considered part of sacred Scripture, inspired by the Holy Spirit, so we can be assured of their teachings.

Now, on to the letter itself.

Introduction: Called by the Grace of God. Paul begins his letter with an uplifting introduction (Ephesians 1:1-2) that, while short, unveils some of the major themes of the whole letter. First, he attributes his apostleship to "the will of God" (1:1). Indeed, Paul later explains in more than one section that we are all called by God for some specific purpose or vocation. Paul next identifies the recipients of the letter as "the faithful in Christ Jesus" (1:1). This description suggests the unity of the faithful in Christ himself, a theme that Paul develops throughout the letter.

Next, Paul uses a unique blessing to set the joyous and thankful tone of the letter (Ephesians 1:3-14). These verses cover salvation history and almost sound like a hymn or a psalm or perhaps an early Christian creed. In it, Paul blesses God, who blessed us humans by choosing to enter into a holy, covenantal relationship with us even before the world began. Then God bestowed further grace upon us through his divine plan of redemption in Christ's death, with our baptism in the Holy Spirit representing the first stage of that redemption. In this way, Paul lays the foundation for the rest of the letter by highlighting the loving relationship between us and God the Father, Jesus his Son, and the Holy Spirit.

Paul closes his introduction with a thanksgiving to God where he praises the Ephesians' faith in Christ and their love for other Christians (Ephesians 1:15-23). He especially emphasizes the mutual nature of our relationship with God. Namely, as we grow in our knowledge of God through faith, God responds by opening our hearts and giving us even more knowledge. While this idea sounds a bit general here, Paul explains it in more detail in the rest of the letter.

The Gift of Salvation. In the main part or body of the letter (Ephesians 2:1–6:20), Paul expands on these major themes. It will be helpful to consider smaller sections of material devoted to a particular theme. To begin, Paul further explains what he means by God's plan of our salvation (2:1-10). These verses can sound rather cosmic and lofty, but basically Paul is speaking to all Christians of what God has done for us in a very real way. Even though we sin and can be enslaved to the things of this world and the desires of our fallen nature—all of which produce a kind of death—God's mercy and love bring us back to life through the death and resurrection of Christ. God didn't have to do this for us. Rather, it was a gift of his grace. Therefore, Paul says, salvation does not come from us, but "by grace you have been saved through faith" (2:8). In response to this gift, our faith should encourage us to do good works.

With God's gift of salvation, we all come together in Christ (Ephesians 2:11-22). Paul notes that through Christ, the original covenant made with the Jews alone (signified by circumcision) now extends to everyone. By bringing us together, Jesus also brought peace. Thus, despite our different backgrounds and cultures, we are all "fellow citizens"—an important claim for the original audience during the time of the Roman Empire—and we are all "members of the household of God" (2:19). This household was founded on the apostles and prophets with Jesus as the cornerstone.

Living as Members of the Household of God. In the rest of the letter, Paul returns to his theme that we are all called by God as he describes the various roles we all have as members of God's household (Ephesians 3:1-21). Paul begins with himself, saying that he was given the gift of "stewardship" (3:2), a term that literally means the manager of a household. As an apostle, Paul also has special insight or understanding into the "mystery of Christ" (3:4). He was granted this gift so that, like the original twelve apostles, he could be a minister and announce to the world the divine plan that he spoke of earlier.

Next Paul addresses the Ephesians in a long persuasive section filled with commands to encourage them—and all of us—to live in a way that responds to God's call and reflects our unity in Christ. How precisely should we live? First, we must exercise virtues such as patience and love to promote a unity based on seven elements: the church, the Holy Spirit, hope, the Lord Jesus Christ, faith, baptism, and God the Father (Ephesians 4:2-6). Since this still sounds a bit theoretical, Paul gets even more specific. Jesus bestows grace on each of us in the form of a gift (4:7-11), namely the roles that we all have to play in the church. Some are apostles, some are pastors, and some are teachers, but we all have the same goal: "to prepare the holy ones for the work of ministry, for building the body of Christ" (4:12). Therefore, all Christians have a role to play in building up the church, a process of growth with every individual believer (4:13-15). Again describing the church as the body of Christ, Paul refers to Christ as the head and notes that only when every part is functioning properly can the whole body grow and build itself (4:16). So, we must work together!

Paul continues to explain how to achieve this unity and build the church by using the language of the "old self" and "new self." He explains that with baptism we gain new life in Christ and must now behave in a righteous manner (Ephesians 4:17-24). That behavior is quite demanding, since it involves a definite moral code. Paul says that we should both avoid particular vices, such as lying and anger, and embrace virtues like kindness and forgiveness toward one another, based on the model of God's forgiveness in Christ (4:25–5:1). Jesus can also be a model for our behavior in terms of his willing and loving sacrifice of himself (5:2). Not only does Jesus' example give us the strength to avoid immoral behavior (5:3-5), it also gives us the ability to persevere in our faith and the teachings of the church (5:6-14). Since there are so many threats to our faith, both in Paul's time and our own, Paul warns us to be vigilant and focus on God the Father, Christ Jesus, and the Spirit (5:15-20).

Since Paul has been using the image of the household of God and explaining the role of Christians in that "house," it is only natural that he next addresses the human household. This section (Ephesians 5:21–6:9) represents a "household code" (see others in Colossians, 1 Timothy, Titus, and 1 Peter), a type of discussion also found in ancient Greek, Roman, and Jewish literature concerning the rules for managing a household. These codes were often based on the three main relationships of husband/wife, father/child, and master/slave. (Slavery was part of the economic vitality of ancient society.) Paul, however, explains these relationships in a Christian context based on how to live in Christ. By recalling the Trinitarian model that we are to imitate God's forgiveness (4:32), model Jesus' loving sacrifice in our daily lives (5:2), and be filled with the Holy Spirit (5:18), Paul clarifies what it means for all Christians to be subordinate to one another (5:21): We should freely and lovingly act on behalf of one another.

This mutual self-subordination plays out in all our relationships. For example, based on the analogy of Christ as the head and the church as the body, the husband is called to imitate Christ and the wife the church (Ephesians 5:24-25). What does this signify exactly? The husband should love his wife freely, totally, and sacrificially by always acting in her best interests. In turn, the wife is to respond by accepting his love with respect. The other two sets of relationships stem from this model.

Conclusion: Soldiers of Christ. Paul concludes by giving the Ephesians some final encouragement and prayers. Before his closing comments and wish for peace, love, and grace (Ephesians 6:23-24), he stresses that in order to live as Christians, we must become like soldiers. But our weapon should be the virtue to stand up to the vices that assault us (6:10-17). Our efforts will be made easier if we pray continually for ourselves and for those, like Paul, who preach the gospel (6:18-20). Therefore, Paul has shown all Christians—both his original audience and us now—the love and unity that God's call produces and the way in which we are to respond through our daily lives in Christ.

Ephesians 1:1-10

1 Paul, an apostle of Christ Jesus by the will of God,
To the saints who are in Ephesus and are faithful in Christ Jesus:
2 Grace to you and peace from God our Father and the Lord
Jesus Christ.
3 Blessed be the God and Father of our Lord Jesus Christ, who
has blessed us in Christ with every spiritual blessing in the heavenly places, 4 just as he chose us in Christ before the foundation of
the world to be holy and blameless before him in love. 5 He destined us for adoption as his children through Jesus Christ, according to the good pleasure of his will, 6 to the praise of his glorious
grace that he freely bestowed on us in the Beloved. 7 In him we
have redemption through his blood, the forgiveness of our trespasses, according to the riches of his grace 8 that he lavished on us.
With all wisdom and insight 9 he has made known to us the mystery of his will, according to his good pleasure that he set forth in
Christ, 10 as a plan for the fullness of time, to gather up all things in
him, things in heaven and things on earth.

How do you view your life? In terms of the challenges that you face each day? In terms of your successes and failures in the past? Or, possibly in terms of your hopes and dreams of the future? Wouldn't it be wonderful to be able to see everything all at once: all the lessons you learned from your past, all the things that will unfold in your future, and all the answers to the problems of today? Here, at the beginning of the Letter to the Ephesians, Scripture gives us a glimpse of this bigger picture. It shows us God's grand purposes for us—indeed, his purposes for the whole universe—and how we fit in!

Scripture tells us that we are blessed with *every spiritual blessing* in Christ (Ephesians 1:3). God loves us so much that he wants to share his heavenly life with us. He has known each one of us from the beginning of time, and he calls us all "very good" (Genesis 1:31). He knew everything we would choose and everything that would happen to us. He knows all of our sufferings and joys intimately. He even foresaw the tragedy of evil, but rather than abandon us, he gave us his Son to overcome sin with love. Now, he invites all of us to become his children through Christ.

God has given us everything we need to accept his invitation. Now it is up to us to trust in his plan and respond to him. The only question facing us is whether or not we will surrender to the love of Christ.

Do you feel confident that God loves you, forgives you, and will supply the grace you need to do his will right now and for the rest of the day? Do you trust that he is always ready to listen to whatever problems you have? If not, slowly read over this passage again. Read the words as if they were written directly to you by your Father. Then, turn with your doubts and concerns to this God who knows and loves you.

"Lord, I worship and praise you for lavishing your grace on your church. I trust in your love, and I thank you for all the blessings you have given me. By your Spirit, I want to share these blessings with everyone I meet today."

Ephesians 1:11-14

11 In Christ we have also obtained an inheritance, having been
destined according to the purpose of him who accomplishes all
things according to his counsel and will, 12 so that we, who were
the first to set our hope on Christ, might live for the praise of his

glory. [13] In him you also, when you had heard the word of truth, the gospel of your salvation, and had believed in him, were marked with the seal of the promised Holy Spirit; [14] this is the pledge of our inheritance toward redemption as God's own people, to the praise of his glory.

Picture this. A letter from an attorney arrives in the mail informing you that your long-lost Uncle Herbert has died, leaving you an immense estate. Is this a hoax, you wonder? But the envelope contains a check for $10,000, a "small first installment, in advance of the full amount, which will be remitted soon." Your estimate of the authenticity of the letter would certainly go up when you cashed the check!

This imaginary exercise does not actually represent how inheritances are handled, but it does convey a sense of what St. Paul meant when he wrote that the Holy Spirit is "the pledge of our inheritance toward redemption as God's own people, to the praise of his glory" (Ephesians 1:14). Paul was using legal terminology to help us understand that the Holy Spirit is the pledge, or "earnest money," of our heavenly inheritance, the first installment of our eternal life with God. Like the first installment, which we can spend while we wait for the balance, the Spirit is available to us now, in our everyday experience. We do not have to wait until we die to share in the inheritance that Christ won for us through his death and resurrection. We can already tap into the life of the Spirit. (Cash that check now!)

Every day, the Spirit is looking for ways to draw us more deeply into the life of the Trinity. He wants to open our eyes to God's love. He helps us recognize God's presence in the kindness and generosity of other people, to be awed by God's greatness displayed in the wonders of the earth and heavens. He accompanies us as we read Scripture, enabling us to receive God's revelation of himself and his plan.

If we listen, we will hear the Spirit speaking in our hearts, calling us to turn away from sin. He will whisper counsel in our ears about how to care for our children and how to deal with difficulties. He will make himself known to us in someone's warm greeting or in a loved one's kiss. He will empower us to reach out to a person in need. When we suffer, he will inspire our prayer and will bring us comfort, healing, and grace.

"Holy Spirit, I welcome you into my life as the down payment of what awaits me in heaven. I ask you to work powerfully in me and through me today."

Ephesians 1:15-23

15 I have heard of your faith in the Lord Jesus and your love toward
all the saints, and for this reason 16 I do not cease to give thanks for
you as I remember you in my prayers. 17 I pray that the God of our
Lord Jesus Christ, the Father of glory, may give you a spirit of wisdom
and revelation as you come to know him, 18 so that, with the eyes of
your heart enlightened, you may know what is the hope to which he
has called you, what are the riches of his glorious inheritance among
the saints, 19 and what is the immeasurable greatness of his power for
us who believe, according to the working of his great power. 20 God
put this power to work in Christ when he raised him from the dead
and seated him at his right hand in the heavenly places, 21 far above
all rule and authority and power and dominion, and above every
name that is named, not only in this age but also in the age to come.

22 And he has put all things under his feet and has made him the
head over all things for the church, 23 which is his body, the fullness
of him who fills all in all.

So many superlatives—"immeasurable greatness," "far above all rule," "all in all"—can boggle the mind. Yet, because of the limitations of human language, even these words are not sufficient to express the impact of Jesus' resurrection. As the Spirit writes these words on our hearts, our vision can expand dramatically. We can begin to *experience* this all-surpassing power at work in our lives. But even then, we remain limited. We will never fully comprehend all that God has accomplished in the resurrection of his Son.

Nevertheless, these words do reflect some of the indescribable power God showed when Jesus' resurrection shook the cosmos. Imagine standing right in the center of an atomic explosion. You would not walk away from that event unchanged. Yet even the effects of an atom bomb are limited to one geographic area and a specific point in time. Jesus' resurrection transformed all of creation for all time. Nothing is unaffected. Nothing is the same now that Jesus is risen. Just to consider it can fill us with wonder and awe.

The promise held out in Christ's resurrection leads us to hope in Christ no matter what circumstances we face. If we ask the Spirit to open our "spiritual eyes"—even if only for a few minutes of prayer each day—we will begin to grasp the immeasurable greatness of Christ's power. We have only to consent to the Spirit's work in us in order to give the Lord an opportunity to open our hearts to his healing and transforming love.

When we pray like this, we are asking Jesus to make effective in us a power that is already at work in the world. The work is done; the victory has already been won. To receive it, we must become vessels of grace, emptied of sin and darkness and open to receive new creation. When we unite ourselves in faith to Jesus' saving work, the river of divine life is released to flow in our hearts. Because Christ is all in all, we can deal with everything that comes our way. As our faith increases, we come to learn that everything that happens in our lives is permitted by the Lord to give us the opportunity to know Christ more fully and to trust him more deeply.

"Lord Jesus, reveal to me the power of your resurrection today. Help me to open my heart to everything you want to give me in your love."

Ephesians 2:1-10

1 You were dead through the trespasses and sins 2 in which you
once lived, following the course of this world, following the ruler of
the power of the air, the spirit that is now at work among those who
are disobedient. 3 All of us once lived among them in the passions of
our flesh, following the desires of flesh and senses, and we were by
nature children of wrath, like everyone else. 4 But God, who is rich
in mercy, out of the great love with which he loved us 5 even when
we were dead through our trespasses, made us alive together with
Christ—by grace you have been saved— 6 and raised us up with him
and seated us with him in the heavenly places in Christ Jesus, 7 so
that in the ages to come he might show the immeasurable riches of
his grace in kindness toward us in Christ Jesus. 8 For by grace you
have been saved through faith, and this is not your own doing; it is
the gift of God— 9 not the result of works, so that no one may boast.
10 For we are what he has made us, created in Christ Jesus for good
works, which God prepared beforehand to be our way of life.

Imagine that a person confined for many years in a prison is suddenly released. Freed so abruptly, he would probably adjust to his new liberty only with great difficulty. Everything about him—his ways of thinking, speaking, relating—would be colored by his experience. Now prone to distrust, suspicion, and self-protection to survive, he might not readily adjust to his freedom. He may have been released from his internment, but, still bound by his ordeal, he is not truly free.

A similar darkness and oppression grips the human oppressed by sin: "You were dead through the trespasses and sins in which you once lived, following . . . the spirit that is now at work among those who are disobedient. All of us once lived among them in the passions of our flesh" (Ephesians 2:1-3). But in Christ Jesus we are freed and brought to life: "God, who is rich in mercy . . . made us alive together with Christ" (2:4-5). It is this new life in Christ that can free us from "the desires of flesh and senses" (2:3).

The "flesh" as used here refers to the unrenewed nature in which every human being is born. Like the fear and suspicion embedded in the ex-prisoner, this "flesh" can dominate the believer's mind. Fleshly desires can mean sinful passions like hatred or lust, or they may take less noticeable forms like slight prejudices or yearnings to raise ourselves up at the expense of others. They can sometimes fill us with fears, unwarranted guilt, or a compelling drive to justify ourselves by our achievements.

Christians have always had to face up to the flesh. Archbishop Baldwin of Canterbury (*d.* 1190) wrote:

> Seemingly pious thoughts often arise simply from within a person or are even suggested by the tempter. . . . There are delusive images of true virtue and even of genuine vice which . . . trick the mind into seeing as good what is not

> good and as evil what is not truly evil. All this deception is due to our wretched ignorance, and should be both regretted and feared. (*Treatise*, 6)

Scripture and tradition call us to examine the ways in which we succumb to the "ruler of the power of the air" (Ephesians 2:2), who uses our flesh as a seedbed of temptation. The situation is not black and white, however; we often move between living for Christ and our flesh. God is "rich in mercy" (2:4), and longs for our total redemption even more than we do. Let us accept the Lord's grace to put off our old self and be renewed in his image.

Ephesians 2:11-22

11 So then, remember that at one time you Gentiles by birth,
called "the uncircumcision" by those who are called "the circumcision"—a physical circumcision made in the flesh by human
hands— 12 remember that you were at that time without Christ,
being aliens from the commonwealth of Israel, and strangers to the
covenants of promise, having no hope and without God in the
world. 13 But now in Christ Jesus you who once were far off have
been brought near by the blood of Christ. 14 For he is our peace; in
his flesh he has made both groups into one and has broken down
the dividing wall, that is, the hostility between us. 15 He has abol-
ished the law with its commandments and ordinances, that he
might create in himself one new humanity in place of the two, thus
making peace, 16 and might reconcile both groups to God in one
body through the cross, thus putting to death that hostility through
it. 17 So he came and proclaimed peace to you who were far off and

peace to those who were near; [18] for through him both of us have access in one Spirit to the Father. [19] So then you are no longer strangers and aliens, but you are citizens with the saints and also members of the household of God, [20] built upon the foundation of the apostles and prophets, with Christ Jesus himself as the cornerstone. [21] In him the whole structure is joined together and grows into a holy temple in the Lord; [22] in whom you also are built together spiritually into a dwelling place for God.

It is difficult to imagine two more fundamentally opposed groups than the Jews and Gentiles at the time of Christ. The Jews, of course, understood themselves to be the chosen people of God. They had received the Law of Moses and were covenanted to God as his special possession. The Gentiles, on the other hand, were considered alienated from the Law, strangers to the covenant, and without God. The wall dividing these two groups was enormous.

Such an animosity, however, posed no problem for Jesus. In his own body, he bore the pain of division and reconciled all of us to the Father, "putting to death that hostility" (Ephesians 2:16). This happened, not only in theory but also in reality, in places like Antioch, Ephesus, and even Rome itself, where Jews and Gentiles came together as one body to worship the Lord, serve one another in love, and proclaim the gospel to the world.

If God could make peace between Jews and Gentiles, how much more can he bring healing and unity in the midst of the divisions we see today? The relative with whom we have not spoken in ages because of a long past hurt? The friend who has drifted away over the years after a misunderstanding? The loved one who has done us wrong and against whom we are bitterly resentful?

In order for us to be freed from our heartaches, we must do as Jesus did and forgive those who have hurt us—no matter how bad the situation may seem. They may not ask our forgiveness. We may not be able to speak to them face to face. Still, if we ensure that our hearts are right before the Lord, he can do wonders. He can even effect miraculous healings and reconciliation. We can all be transformed as Jesus' merciful heart takes deeper root in us. The keys are prayer and forgiveness. As we spend time with Jesus in prayer, he can set our hearts right with regard to particular situations. He will give us his love so that we can give it to others.

"Lord Jesus, no matter how justified I may feel, for your sake, I freely forgive everyone who has ever hurt me. I do not want to hold anyone bound by my lack of mercy. Lord, bring healing and reconciliation."

Ephesians 3:1-13

1 This is the reason that I Paul am a prisoner for Christ Jesus for
the sake of you Gentiles— 2 for surely you have already heard of the
commission of God's grace that was given me for you, 3 and how the
mystery was made known to me by revelation, as I wrote above in a
few words, 4 a reading of which will enable you to perceive my understanding of the mystery of Christ. 5 In former generations this mystery was not made known to humankind, as it has now been revealed
to his holy apostles and prophets by the Spirit: 6 that is, the Gentiles
have become fellow heirs, members of the same body, and sharers in
the promise in Christ Jesus through the gospel.
7 Of this gospel I have become a servant according to the gift of
God's grace that was given me by the working of his power.
8 Although I am the very least of all the saints, this grace was
given to me to bring to the Gentiles the news of the boundless

riches of Christ, [9] and to make everyone see what is the plan of the mystery hidden for ages in God who created all things; [10] so that through the church the wisdom of God in its rich variety might now be made known to the rulers and authorities in the heavenly places. [11] This was in accordance with the eternal purpose that he has carried out in Christ Jesus our Lord, [12] in whom we have access to God in boldness and confidence through faith in him. [13] I pray therefore that you may not lose heart over my sufferings for you; they are your glory.

God's grace reaches so far beyond our understanding that it lifts us off our feet. According to St. Paul, God's plan—the mystery of his working through Christ which was kept hidden for ages—has now been revealed by the Holy Spirit (Ephesians 3:2-5). What was that plan? To bring all things together in Christ, even to the point of reconciling Jew and Gentile, through the blood that Jesus shed on the cross (2:13-16). Evidently, God's love and grace were intended not only for Israel but for all humanity.

The church is the world reconciled, the place where humanity rediscovers its lost unity. According to the *Catechism of the Catholic Church*, in order to accomplish his plan "to reunite all his children, scattered and led astray by sin, the Father willed to call the whole of humanity together into his Son's Church" (CCC, 845). The church is meant to be God's representative to all the nations of the world, the universal sign and instrument of salvation.

We are all members of this church, and we have all been entrusted with this ministry of reconciliation and unity. We exercise our ministry more powerfully as we grow in love for all our brothers and sisters in

Christ. When we put aside animosity and prejudice against brothers and sisters who belong to other churches and denominations, we deal a serious blow to the devil's plans to divide humanity and obscure God's mercy. We bear witness to the world that God can truly heal every single division and wound from which our fallen race suffers.

Let's forgive those who have injured us so that we can break down the dividing walls of hostility that keep the church from shining in this darkened world. Jesus told his disciples that when Christians love one another and live in unity, the world will take notice and recognize that God has sent his Son to redeem it (John 17:21-23). May the Holy Spirit give us new grace for loving our brothers and sisters in Christ, and fresh hope for Christian unity.

"Lord Jesus, make us truly one, as you and the Father are one. Let us know the power of your love so that we may be instruments of your peace to all around us."

Ephesians 3:14-21

14 For this reason I bow my knees before the Father, 15 from whom
every family in heaven and on earth takes its name. 16 I pray that,
according to the riches of his glory, he may grant that you may be
strengthened in your inner being with power through his Spirit,
17 and that Christ may dwell in your hearts through faith, as you are
being rooted and grounded in love. 18 I pray that you may have the
power to comprehend, with all the saints, what is the breadth and
length and height and depth, 19 and to know the love of Christ that
surpasses knowledge, so that you may be filled with all the fullness
of God.

[20] Now to him who by the power at work within us is able to accomplish abundantly far more than all we can ask or imagine, [21] to him be glory in the church and in Christ Jesus to all generations, forever and ever. Amen.

Jesus died on the cross for us so that every day we could share more fully in an inner, personal relationship with the triune God. This is God's work inside us, an outpouring of love that continually transforms us into his likeness, day after day. It is not something we earn by our good deeds. Rather, as God touches our lives we turn from sin and conform ourselves to the model of Jesus, our gracious Redeemer.

Modern technological society tends to make us look at ourselves—and our needs—superficially. Everything seems geared toward comfort and ease. The root of much of the alcoholism and drug abuse we witness is the desire to escape the demands of life in search of a state of mind where everything is calm and peaceful. Many people live as if all their problems and fears could be allayed through the amassing of material possessions and greater financial security.

Such thinking tends to reduce the gospel to a series of commands or suggestions for doing "the right thing." The concern is to avoid hell and "make it" to heaven—while still enjoying as much of the pleasures of this earthly life as we can. Paul, however, didn't pray for God to change our external behavior so that we appear less sinful. He prayed that we would know God's love personally, in the depths of our being, and that this love would transform us completely, from the inside out.

God's purposes for us involve an ever-increasing revelation of Jesus Christ in our hearts, an ever-deepening awareness of his grace at work within us. The Christian life is meant to be dynamic and active, bringing us into Christ's life more fully every day. We are not called simply to do good deeds, but to let our lives bear witness to the power of the Spirit. As God's love is opened up to us, sin will naturally fall away. God's wisdom will fill us to such an extent that even our smallest deeds will testify to the power of the new life within us.

"Heavenly Father, I bow down to you in praise and gratitude for your plan for me. By your Spirit, help me each day to know more fully your love, which is able to 'accomplish abundantly far more than all we can ask or imagine' (Ephesians 3:20). Jesus, I want to become like you."

Ephesians 4:1-6

1 I therefore, the prisoner in the Lord, beg you to lead a life worthy
of the calling to which you have been called, 2 with all humility and
gentleness, with patience, bearing with one another in love, 3 making
every effort to maintain the unity of the Spirit in the bond of peace.
4 There is one body and one Spirit, just as you were called to the one
hope of your calling, 5 one Lord, one faith, one baptism, 6 one God
and Father of all, who is above all and through all and in all.

Because God is perfect goodness, his work in us and his plan for us must be magnificent as well. The desire of his heart for his children flows out of his infinite love. In light of this truth, Paul called us to "lead a life worthy of the calling to which you have been called" (Ephesians 4:1).

What is this calling? It is an invitation to walk in holiness and humility, to be vessels of God's grace, united with one another in love under the headship of Jesus Christ. This high calling is for *all* of God's sons and daughters, not just a few. It is not something we can earn; it is a gift from our heavenly Father, who promises to lead us day by day in our life with him.

Paul proclaimed the "oneness" of everything under God: "One body and one Spirit, . . . one hope, . . . one Lord, . . . one faith, one baptism, one God and Father of all" (Ephesians 4:4-6). It is thought that these "oneness" proclamations may have originally been acclamations used in early Christian baptismal liturgies. Catechumens, about to be baptized, might have made such statements as a profession of faith and a commitment to uphold the unity of the body to which they were about to be joined.

What a magnificent call from the Lord! As we come to understand the great dignity of the life we have received, we will be moved to ask the Lord to fill us with his grace and to heal all divisions. God never intended for us to rely solely on our own resources, but to receive his grace to help us every day. Only he can transform us and secure the unity of his church that he so longs to see. Only his love can cover a multitude of sins. Only his power can break down the walls that divide us. What hope this holds out for us!

As we seek to grow in Christ, let us recall the grace that is available to us. We have a precious call as sons and daughters of God. May the Father's heart become our heart. May we all pray for unity among all believers so that the church would shine as a bright witness to the life of Christ.

Ephesians 4:7-16

7 But each of us was given grace according to the measure of
Christ's gift. 8 Therefore it is said,

> "When he ascended on high he made captivity itself a captive;
> he gave gifts to his people."

9 (When it says, "He ascended," what does it mean but that he had
also descended into the lower parts of the earth? 10 He who
descended is the same one who ascended far above all the heavens,
so that he might fill all things.) 11 The gifts he gave were that some
would be apostles, some prophets, some evangelists, some pastors
and teachers, 12 to equip the saints for the work of ministry, for
building up the body of Christ, 13 until all of us come to the unity of
the faith and of the knowledge of the Son of God, to maturity, to
the measure of the full stature of Christ. 14 We must no longer be
children, tossed to and fro and blown about by every wind of doctrine, by people's trickery, by their craftiness in deceitful scheming.
15 But speaking the truth in love, we must grow up in every way
into him who is the head, into Christ, 16 from whom the whole
body, joined and knit together by every ligament with which it is
equipped, as each part is working properly, promotes the body's
growth in building itself up in love.

I don't have any." That may be the answer many of us give when asked to list our gifts. But this passage from Ephesians tells us that God has given each of us gifts that equip us for the work of ministry, for building up the body of Christ. How do you go about identifying your natural gifts? Thinking about what you like to do or what you can do well provides a clue. And even if you have already discovered many of your gifts, stay alert: New ones become apparent as time goes on.

In addition to our natural gifts and talents, God loves to see us develop the *supernatural* gifts he has given us, gifts like healing and extraordinary faith. This doesn't mean we have to stand on the corner with a "Repent!" sign, or confront the president with a word of prophecy! In fact, supernatural gifts can often look quite mundane at first, as they develop out of our natural abilities.

Say, for example, that you bring some of your famous chicken soup over to a sick neighbor, but then hear the Spirit nudging you to pray with her for healing. You may be experiencing both natural and supernatural gifts. Or perhaps God fine-tunes your natural inclination to be a positive-thinking person by giving you the supernatural gift of encouragement. Led by the Lord, you step out in faith and speak a particular message to someone. Obeying such a prompting can make you part of God's perfect timing for that person.

Take another example from ordinary life: Let God form you in the patience required to deal with children, and you allow him to transform your gift of parenting. Even common sense can become a supernatural gift when it is based on inspired applications of the counsel to "train children in the right way" (Proverbs 22:6).

Whether natural or supernatural, our gifts come from God, who wants us to develop them for the sake of the church. It's exciting to think of the things we can do for God. Even taking our everyday tasks and filling them with God's presence can result in the miraculous. Why? Because Christ is in us!

"Lord Jesus, you equip me with gifts and talents to help build your body. Show me how to play my part, and remove my fear of letting you have your way."

Ephesians 4:17-24

17 Now this I affirm and insist on in the Lord: you must no longer
live as the Gentiles live, in the futility of their minds. 18 They are
darkened in their understanding, alienated from the life of God
because of their ignorance and hardness of heart. 19 They have lost
all sensitivity and have abandoned themselves to licentiousness,
greedy to practice every kind of impurity. 20 That is not the way you
learned Christ! 21 For surely you have heard about him and were
taught in him, as truth is in Jesus. 22 You were taught to put away
your former way of life, your old self, corrupt and deluded by its
lusts, 23 and to be renewed in the spirit of your minds, 24 and to
clothe yourselves with the new self, created according to the likeness of God in true righteousness and holiness.

Have you ever seen a snake shed? When its old skin becomes shrunken and wrinkled and begins to stink, the snake will seek a place where two stones lie close together and then force itself through the tight spot to rip off the aged membrane. Underneath, a fresh, new skin is revealed.

Paul frequently used a similar metaphor to illustrate the spiritual transformation God works in us through the Holy Spirit: We are to strip or "put away" our old selves and and "be renewed in the spirit of your minds," one that is "created according to the likeness of God" (Ephesians 4:22-24). Although humans don't shed skin in the way a snake does, we are nonetheless called to "put on the Lord Jesus Christ, and make no provision for the flesh" (Romans 13:14). Other English translations of this biblical image encourage the believer, "Clothe yourself in Christ" or "Put on Christ like a garment." *The New Testament in Modern English*, a paraphrased English-language version by J. B. Phillips, makes Paul's point particularly clear: "Fling off the dirty clothes of the old way of living, which were rotted through and through . . . put on the clean fresh clothes of the new life which was made by God's design for righteousness and the holiness which is no illusion."

This transition from the life of sin to the life of grace begins at our baptism and is meant to continue through the rest of our lives (Romans 6:3-11). In the baptismal ceremony—which would have been very familiar to Paul's readers who were largely newly baptized believers—new Christians put on a white garment as a visual expression of the profound spiritual change that had taken place in them. "We are clothed," wrote St. John of Avila, "and the clothing we are given is not just something beautiful and costly: It is Jesus Christ himself, who is the sum total of all beauty, all value, all richness." Because this baptismal transformation involves putting on Christ himself, it is not simply an external alteration akin to changing our clothes. Rather, it is an interior renewal that has the potential to make us an entirely new creation (2 Corinthians 5:17).

With the "so then" coming up in the next line of his letter (Ephesians 4:25), Paul will tell the Ephesians—and us—exactly what this new nature "created according to the likeness of God in true righteous and holiness" (4:24) should look like.

"Thank you, Lord Jesus, for making me a new creation. Help me, through the grace of my baptism, to put aside my old ways so that you may complete your work of transforming me into your own likeness."

Ephesians 4:25-32

25 So then, putting away falsehood, let all of us speak the truth to
our neighbors, for we are members of one another. 26 Be angry but
do not sin; do not let the sun go down on your anger, 27 and do not
make room for the devil. 28 Thieves must give up stealing; rather let
them labor and work honestly with their own hands, so as to have
something to share with the needy. 29 Let no evil talk come out of
your mouths, but only what is useful for building up, as there is
need, so that your words may give grace to those who hear. 30 And
do not grieve the Holy Spirit of God, with which you were marked
with a seal for the day of redemption. 31 Put away from you all bit-
terness and wrath and anger and wrangling and slander, together
with all malice, 32 and be kind to one another, tenderhearted, for-
giving one another, as God in Christ has forgiven you.

So then . . . (*Ephesians 4:25*)

Earlier in his letter to the Christians in Ephesus, Paul explained how God made them new men and women by reconciling them to himself through Christ (Ephesians 2:15-16). Then he reminded them that they had put aside their old natures, which belonged to their former sinful manner of life, and that their new natures reflected the likeness in which they were newly created—the likeness of God himself (4:22-24). *So then*, he reasoned, this profound spiritual transformation—a transformation that took place through baptism—should be evident in their new ways of behaving.

Following this reasoning further, Paul arrived at the logical consequence of this transformation: Christ's followers should be distinguishable from non-Christians. The Ephesians were to "no longer live as the Gentiles live" (Ephesians 4:17). They were not to follow worldly standards or exhibit the same behavior patterns as those in the society around them, especially to the extent that this society was characterized by deceit, greed, and other sinful practices.

Christians are to reflect God's righteousness in their way of living. Thus, Paul's *so then* in verse 25 prefaces more than a dozen concise directives to the Ephesians—and us—showing how to do this: Don't tell lies. Speak the truth. Be careful not to sin when you are angry. Don't steal. Do honest work and give to those in need. Cut out the bad language. Watch the tongue. Let go of bitter grudges. Don't be malicious. Be kind. (Ephesians 4:25-32). Paul's words here are quite clear and down-to-earth. When we resist cheating to get a good deal at work, when we remain patient and loving with our children even when they exasperate us, or when we refuse to gossip in the office or across the back fence, we are putting these exhortations concretely into practice. As varied as Paul's directives are, they all point to an upright life lived in love—and point us toward protecting our unity as "members of one another," members of the body of Christ (4:25).

When we feel challenged by Paul's high call, all we need to do is recall that we have been baptized into Christ and filled with his Holy Spirit. It is no longer we who live but Christ who lives in us (Galatians 2:20). Let's not forget that we are God's workmanship, created in Christ Jesus for good works, which God prepared beforehand, that we should walk in them (Ephesians 2:10). *So then . . .*

"Lord Jesus, let me know the intimacy with you and the power over sin that are part of my new life in you. By your Spirit, help me hold fast to this new life and to do everything I can to help it grow and take deeper root in me."

Ephesians 5:1-8

1 Therefore be imitators of God, as beloved children, 2 and live
in love, as Christ loved us and gave himself up for us, a fragrant
offering and sacrifice to God.
3 But fornication and impurity of any kind, or greed, must not
even be mentioned among you, as is proper among saints. 4 Entirely
out of place is obscene, silly, and vulgar talk; but instead, let there
be thanksgiving. 5 Be sure of this, that no fornicator or impure person, or one who is greedy (that is, an idolater), has any inheritance
in the kingdom of Christ and of God.
6 Let no one deceive you with empty words, for because of these
things the wrath of God comes on those who are disobedient.
7 Therefore do not be associated with them. 8 For once you were
darkness, but now in the Lord you are light.

St. Paul told the Christians in Ephesus to "live" in love (Ephesians 5:2). For some, that expression may conjure up a vague and difficult goal. For others it may sound like a call to be syrupy sweet all the time. But St. Paul had a very practical, realistic concept of love.

For Paul, loving doesn't just mean having pleasant feelings for people. It does involve being kind and compassionate, pure and honest toward others (Ephesians 4:32; 5:3-5). But it also means serving other people as Christ has served us (5:1-2). It means living a life consecrated to the Lord in obedience to his commands. One who loves in Christ understands that living by obedience and truth helps keep us stable and enables us to fix our eyes on the goal of becoming vessels of Christ to everyone we meet.

In our culture, love is considered a feeling, something over which we have no control. We either love someone or we don't. Love just happens. But God demonstrates love very differently. Certainly, Jesus did not "feel" like dying an agonizing death on the cross. But he chose to obey his Father and gave his life as a sacrifice. This is the greatest demonstration of true love.

Love also recognizes limits. As a loving Father, God has marked out boundaries for us, boundaries that help us distinguish between what is loving and what is not (Ephesians 5:5-8). Just as children appreciate the boundaries set by their parents, our Father in heaven wants us to embrace the boundaries he has set for us—the wisdom of his commands.

Let us pray that as we walk in love as Jesus did, the witness of our lives will reach the people around us with the promise of truth and salvation. Let us pray that our obedience to God and our service to others will bring God's light into the midst of the darkness and sin so prevalent today. Most of all, let us pray that through us God's tender love will become visible to everyone we meet.

"Father, I want to choose to love the people around me. Let your love flow out to others through me. Help me to live in love in a way that not only makes people feel better, but leads them to you and brings honor to your name."

Ephesians 5:8-20

8 Live as children of light— 9 for the fruit of the light is found in
all that is good and right and true. 10 Try to find out what is pleasing to the Lord. 11 Take no part in the unfruitful works of darkness,
but instead expose them. 12 For it is shameful even to mention what
such people do secretly; 13 but everything exposed by the light
becomes visible, 14 for everything that becomes visible is light.
Therefore it says,

"Sleeper, awake!
Rise from the dead,
and Christ will shine on you."

15 Be careful then how you live, not as unwise people but as wise,
16 making the most of the time, because the days are evil. 17 So do
not be foolish, but understand what the will of the Lord is. 18 Do
not get drunk with wine, for that is debauchery; but be filled with
the Spirit, 19 as you sing psalms and hymns and spiritual songs
among yourselves, singing and making melody to the Lord in your
hearts, 20 giving thanks to God the Father at all times and for
everything in the name of our Lord Jesus Christ.

Recently, a man made the headlines when he came out of a nineteen-year-long coma. Upon waking up, his first words were, "Mom . . . Pepsi . . . milk." The man was astonished by the world into which he woke: The Berlin Wall is gone; Ronald Reagan is no longer president; and cyberspace is filled with e-mail messages that reach the other side of the world almost instantly. He has left behind the darkness in which his mind had been sleeping, and now he is entering into a new life—and gaining a new perspective on reality.

Like this man who woke out of his coma, Christians come, through baptism, out of the "sleep of death" into a new existence—life in a new world illuminated by Christ. Paul vividly described the contrast between the bright clarity a person obtains when he awakens from a deep sleep and the profound darkness experienced by one who remains asleep. "Sleeper, awake! Rise from the dead, and Christ will shine on you" (Ephesians 5:14). With these rousing words of what was, most likely, a hymn used in the early church's baptismal liturgy, he reminded the Ephesians—recently baptized believers—that they had been awakened from the sleep of a spiritual death and raised to newness of life in the risen Christ.

As baptized Christians, we live in the light of Christ. This "light" involves a good understanding of what God has done for us: "He has rescued us from the power of darkness and transferred us into the kingdom of his beloved Son, in whom we have redemption, the forgiveness of sins" (Colossians 1:13-14).

As we let Jesus' truth enlighten our minds and hearts, we find that we no longer have to take part in "the unfruitful works of darkness" (Ephesians 5:11). Instead, we discover that we really can know "what is pleasing to the Lord" (5:10). Permeated by the light of Christ, we are empowered to live not as the unwise or foolish do but in a new way, understanding God's will for us (5:15-17). On our own, we may stumble around in darkness, but we have been "filled with the Spirit" (5:18), and that Spirit really does have the power to raise us to live in the light.

"Father, how grateful I am that you have raised me up to new life in your Son, Jesus! Help me to cast off any remnants of sin and darkness that still cling to me. I want to produce 'the fruit of the light found in all that is good and right and true' (Ephesians 5:9)."

Ephesians 5:21-33

21 Be subject to one another out of reverence for Christ.
22 Wives, be subject to your husbands as you are to the Lord.
23 For the husband is the head of the wife just as Christ is the head
of the church, the body of which he is the Savior. 24 Just as the
church is subject to Christ, so also wives ought to be, in everything,
to their husbands.
25 Husbands, love your wives, just as Christ loved the church and
gave himself up for her, 26 in order to make her holy by cleansing
her with the washing of water by the word, 27 so as to present the
church to himself in splendor, without a spot or wrinkle or anything of the kind—yes, so that she may be holy and without blemish. 28 In the same way, husbands should love their wives as they do
their own bodies. He who loves his wife loves himself. 29 For no one
ever hates his own body, but he nourishes and tenderly cares for it,
just as Christ does for the church, 30 because we are members of his
body. 31 "For this reason a man will leave his father and mother and
be joined to his wife, and the two will become one flesh." 32 This is
a great mystery, and I am applying it to Christ and the church.
33 Each of you, however, should love his wife as himself, and a wife
should respect her husband.

Jesus' relationship with the church is our model for married life. Husbands are to love their wives, "as Christ loved the church and gave himself up for her" (Ephesians 5:25). Out of love for us, Jesus gave up his own life to redeem us. He did not consider his position with the Father as something to hold on to selfishly while we remained lost in sin. Rather, laying aside his glory, he humbled himself and allowed himself to be crucified for us so that we might be redeemed (Philippians 2:6-7). This was the extent to which God the Son was willing to go in order to rescue us and unite us as his bride, his church.

Very few of us are called to die for our husbands or our wives. Yet every day, in so many ways, we have opportunities to serve one another, laying down our own concerns for the sake of our spouse's needs. Because Christian marriage is a participation in the mystery of Jesus' love for the church, every act of self-sacrifice that husbands and wives make for each other can be elevated to a wonderful, life-changing height.

As we sacrifice ourselves and our desires for one another, we actually participate in the life of Christ, the perfect servant of God, who laid down his life for us all. As we ask the Spirit to enable us to love as Jesus did, we will see attitudes of reluctance and selfishness give way to a heartfelt desire, even an eagerness, to care for one another. God delights in giving us the grace to become more like his Son; he only waits for us to ask him.

In his letter to the Philippians, Paul tells us that because Jesus humbled himself, God raised him high, giving him authority over all creation (Philippians 2:8-10). As we give up our lives for one another, we too will be raised up with Christ. As servants of Christ and of one another, we will know a dignity and authority that far surpasses the false self-esteem that comes from grasping for power and importance. It is in the family first and foremost that we learn that those who serve are the most free of all.

"Jesus, may the love that burns in your heart for the church move us to serve and love those in our family so that we can be a living testimony to your unconditional love."

Ephesians 6:1-9

1 Children, obey your parents in the Lord, for this is right.
2 "Honor your father and mother"—this is the first commandment
with a promise: 3 "so that it may be well with you and you may live
long on the earth."
4 And, fathers, do not provoke your children to anger, but bring
them up in the discipline and instruction of the Lord.
5 Slaves, obey your earthly masters with fear and trembling, in
singleness of heart, as you obey Christ; 6 not only while being
watched, and in order to please them, but as slaves of Christ, doing
the will of God from the heart. 7 Render service with enthusiasm,
as to the Lord and not to men and women, 8 knowing that whatever good we do, we will receive the same again from the Lord,
whether we are slaves or free.
9 And, masters, do the same to them. Stop threatening them, for
you know that both of you have the same Master in heaven, and
with him there is no partiality.

The Letter to the Ephesians, with its advice to slaves and masters (Ephesians 6:5-9), was written during a period when at least one out of every three people in the Roman Empire was a slave. Slavery was an accepted institution that supported the social and economic structures of the culture. Slaves were considered mere tools of their masters and had no personal rights under the law. Since slave owners exercised absolute mastery over their human property, some slaves were subjected to vicious cruelty.

In his work with the church in Ephesus—which included slaves and slave owners alike—Paul never addressed the institution of slavery directly; he neither endorsed it nor advocated its overthrow by violence. He had a different objective: to enlighten everyone about the fundamental dignity of every human person. Since both slave and master "have the same Master in heaven" (Ephesians 6:9), they are both free agents and equal in status in God's eyes. Paul directed slaves to see themselves as children and heirs of God and to do their work for the Lord and for the reward they could expect from him. This perspective opened the way to an eventual rethinking of the institution of slavery, even as it gave oppressed slaves an immediate sense of dignity and purpose.

Also revolutionary was Paul's assertion that within the Christian household, slaves had rights, and masters had a responsibility to treat them with justice and kindness. In his letter to Philemon, Paul even appeals to the Christian owner of a runaway slave, asking him to welcome the man back "no longer as a slave but more than a slave, a beloved brother" (Philemon 16)!

While the spread of Christianity did not immediately lead to the abolition of slavery, it set in motion the forces that eventually resulted in the widespread freeing of slaves. Today, in Sudan and other parts of the world, hundreds of thousands of people are enslaved. Let's do all we can to fight this injustice while praying that more and more people will take on the mind of Christ, which changes the world by changing hearts.

"Lord Jesus, we pray for the end of slavery. Comfort all who are abused in this way. Holy Spirit, convict slave owners of sin, and send them messages of your gospel."

Ephesians 6:10-20

10 Finally, be strong in the Lord and in the strength of his power.
11 Put on the whole armor of God, so that you may be able to stand
against the wiles of the devil. 12 For our struggle is not against enemies of blood and flesh, but against the rulers, against the authorities, against the cosmic powers of this present darkness, against the
spiritual forces of evil in the heavenly places. 13 Therefore take up
the whole armor of God, so that you may be able to withstand on
that evil day, and having done everything, to stand firm. 14 Stand
therefore, and fasten the belt of truth around your waist, and put on
the breastplate of righteousness. 15 As shoes for your feet put on
whatever will make you ready to proclaim the gospel of peace.
16 With all of these, take the shield of faith, with which you will be
able to quench all the flaming arrows of the evil one. 17 Take the
helmet of salvation, and the sword of the Spirit, which is the word
of God.
18 Pray in the Spirit at all times in every prayer and supplication.
To that end keep alert and always persevere in supplication for all
the saints. 19 Pray also for me, so that when I speak, a message may
be given to me to make known with boldness the mystery of the
gospel, 20 for which I am an ambassador in chains. Pray that I may
declare it boldly, as I must speak.

Many a fable and story have been built around the adage, "Things are not what they seem." The ugly frog may in fact be a handsome prince. Your most gracious neighbor might actually be a villain, looking for the first opportunity to betray you. Or, the poor carpenter could really be the Son of God who rules legions of warrior-angels. If we judged only by appearances, we would never see people in the fullness of their true light.

This is the principle behind these words about the nature of our battles. So many of the struggles and difficulties in our lives camouflage the fact that—at their foundation—there are spiritual forces of evil. Through lies and insinuations, these malign spirits seek to move us off of our position of faith and trust in God. Too often, however, we blame our struggles on other people or events: "If only he would be more patient, I wouldn't get so upset." "If she didn't get angry, I wouldn't get angry." But why should we become so upset in the first place? If we know we are beloved sons and daughters of God, indwelt and empowered by the Spirit of God, what could possibly threaten us or disturb our tranquility?

Because there are forces of darkness trying to confuse us and turn us from Christ, we must know clearly who we are in Christ. Baptized into his death and resurrection, we have been raised with Jesus to the heavenly realm (Ephesians 2:4-6). Filled with his Spirit, we are now a new creation (2 Corinthians 5:17). Our heritage extends beyond time and space; we have at our disposal all the ammunition of divine truth, God's righteousness, and the living word of God. We are no mere people!

Victory in this spiritual battle will be ours as we learn to take up a position of faith and hold fast to the spiritual life we have received. No Christian should ever go about his or her day under a cloud of defeat or hopelessness. Be quick to turn to the Spirit who dwells in us and ask to be set free. We can know peace and clarity when we ponder the word of God and hold fast to the truths it proclaims. Let us stand first against the wiles of the evil one and pray for each other.

Ephesians 6:21-24

21 So that you also may know how I am and what I am doing,
Tychicus will tell you everything. He is a dear brother and a faithful
minister in the Lord. 22 I am sending him to you for this very purpose, to let you know how we are, and to encourage your hearts.
23 Peace be to the whole community, and love with faith, from
God the Father and the Lord Jesus Christ. 24 Grace be with all who
have an undying love for our Lord Jesus Christ.

Peace. . . . Grace. (Ephesians 6:23,24)

What better sentiments could you offer to someone you love? That's exactly what Paul did in every message that he sent to the early Christian communities. The Letter to the Ephesians ends in the same way that it began: with greetings that invoke God's grace and peace for all those to whom Paul was writing (Ephesians 1:2; 6:23-24). This is the way, too, that he opened and closed almost every one of his other letters.

In the ancient Greco-Roman world, the standard greeting at the beginning of a letter wished the recipient material prosperity or good fortune and good health. The prayerful wishes of Paul's openings, however, far exceeded the typical "best wishes" of the societies that surrounded him. He wished his readers something far greater, something of eternal value: the blessings and gifts of God that come through faith in Christ. The refrain "Grace and peace to you from God our Father and our Lord Jesus Christ" was Paul's own special "Hallmark" greeting, and it has become a hallmark of Christian people everywhere.

With the word "grace," Paul summed up God's mercy and graciousness, which come to us in the form of sanctifying grace and the virtues and gifts of the Holy Spirit. And with the word "peace," he was proclaiming that salvation and all good things, heavenly and earthly, are attainable because Jesus' death and resurrection have removed—once and for all—the enmity between God and man and reconciled us to our heavenly Father (Ephesians 2:4-6,16; see also Romans 5:1; 2 Corinthians 5:18-19; Colossians 1:22). So dear to Paul's heart were the effects of this reconciliation through Christ that the word "peace" is found eight times in this epistle alone!

When we possess this peace of God "which surpasses all understanding" (Philippians 4:7), we have nothing to fear from the difficulties, trials, and sorrows of daily life or from the temptations of the devil. Let's receive Paul's benediction—"Peace be to the whole community. . . . Grace be with all who have an undying love for our Lord Jesus Christ" (Ephesians 6:23-24)—with gratitude, and let's also pray it as a blessing on all who are dear to us.

"Jesus, I thank you for the grace you have given me through the cross. By the power of this grace, may I be filled more and more with peace and hope, even in the midst of trials and difficulties."

Building the Church through Humility and Service

The Letter to the Philippians

An Introduction to the Letter to the Philippians

by Fr. Joseph F. Wimmer, O.S.A.

Philippi was a city in ancient Macedonia, now northern Greece, near the Adriatic Sea, facing Asia Minor (modern Turkey). It had been founded by Philip II, father of Alexander the Great, around 358 B.C., but was conquered by the Romans in 157 B.C., and after the victory of Antony and Octavian there against Brutus and Cassius in 42 B.C., it was given over largely to veterans of the imperial Roman army for settlement. The city was made an official Roman colony (Acts 16:12), and was subject to special Roman law. Its inhabitants were mostly Gentiles of Greek and Roman background, though a small Jewish community resided there as well.

Paul visited Philippi during his second missionary journey, around A.D. 50, and as was his custom, first went to the Jewish people. Apparently they had no synagogue, for on the sabbath they gathered at the edge of the river just outside the city, where Paul and his companions—Timothy, Silas, and Luke—met them and announced the good news about Jesus. One of the women, Lydia, a dealer in purple cloth, accepted Paul's message, was baptized a Christian with her whole household, and persuaded Paul and his friends to stay at her home (Acts 16:13-15).

During his time at Philippi, Paul cured a slave girl of an evil spirit that had allowed her to predict the future. Her owners—who had profited from her fortunetelling—were furious, seized Paul and Silas, and brought them before the Roman officials. Paul and Silas were flogged and thrown into jail. An earthquake that night damaged the prison and would have allowed the prisoners to escape, but at Paul's urging they all remained. The jailer was so impressed he dressed the apostles' wounds, gave them food, and became a Christian with his whole family. Upon learning that Paul and Silas were Roman citizens, the authorities apologized and asked them to leave the city. After gathering once more at Lydia's house with a growing number of believers, they left for Thessalonica to continue their missionary activity (Acts 16:16-40).

Where and Why? Paul wrote his letter to the Philippians while imprisoned, around A.D. 57 (1:13-17), probably toward the end of his three-year ministry in Ephesus (Acts 20:31). Luke does not specifically say that Paul was imprisoned in Ephesus, but he does mention an uprising of the silversmiths there because of Paul's preaching (19:23-41), which might have landed him in jail. Paul states in 1 Corinthians 15:32 that he had to fight "wild beasts" at Ephesus (the silversmiths?), and, in 2 Corinthians 11:23, that he was in prison "more times" than some others, which leaves open the possibility of an imprisonment there. The main reason for thinking he wrote from Ephesus, however, is its closeness to Philippi, which the letter seems to imply. In his conclusion, Paul sends greetings from the "household of Caesar" (Philippians 4:22). The "household of Caesar" is mentioned also in some inscriptions found at Ephesus.

The Philippians had sent Epaphroditus to care for Paul and bring him some gifts. They then heard that Epaphroditus had fallen ill and became worried about him. Paul responds to their kindness and concern with this letter, and uses the occasion to strengthen them in their faith and in their relations with one another. So the letter is divided into three parts: a brief description of Paul's situation while in prison (1:1-26); an exhortation to unity through humility with three examples (1:27–4:3); and a conclusion and expression of gratitude for the gifts sent to him (4:4-23).

Part I: Paul in Prison

Opening Address (1:1-2). According to Hellenistic custom, Paul begins the letter with his name, and that of his companion Timothy, who was known to the Philippians. He addresses them as *hagioi*, "saints." The Israelites had an ancient tradition of being a priestly people (Exodus 19:6), a "holy" people (Leviticus 19:1). Paul transfers this title to the Christians, "saints in Christ Jesus," that is, the people of God sanctified by Christ and called to holiness. He singles out the *episkopoi* and *diakonoi*, translated loosely at this early time as "overseers" and "assistants," perhaps because they were the ones immediately responsible for the gifts brought to him. To them all he wishes "grace and peace" from "God our Father" and "the Lord Jesus Christ." It's interesting to note here the intimate association between Jesus and the Father.

Initial Thanksgiving (1:3-11). Next comes the customary thanksgiving, which Paul transforms into a spiritually uplifting and cordial reaffirmation of his close friendship with them, "thankful for your partnership in the gospel" (Philippians 1:5). The word "partnership," *koinonia*, is an important term for Paul, since it expresses a whole range of shared experiences within the community. It is an indication that Paul's primary audience is always the community, and his goal, that they be a "sharing" community, in true *koinonia*.

This insight is still valid for our churches today. God, who began the "good work" in them, will bring it to completion on judgment day. The Day of Judgment is no longer the Day of the Lord Yahweh as in Amos 5:18 and many other Old Testament passages, but the "Day of Jesus Christ." Jesus is the great judge at the end of the world. Paul's prayer is that as his readers abound in love, they may grow in that closeness with God, and bear the "fruits of righteousness which come through Jesus Christ." The power of grace in their corporate life is profoundly emphasized.

Paul's Imprisonment (1:12-26). Paul tells the Philippians that his imprisonment has resulted in the spreading of the gospel throughout the military guard (praetorium), since they knew that he was imprisoned for the sake of Christ. Others were emboldened to preach the Christian message, some perhaps for questionable motives, but Paul is glad that at least Christ is proclaimed. He also meditates on the significance of his life and possible execution. He would not be worried either way, because as he says, "to me to live is Christ, and to die is gain" (Philippians 1:21). Given a preference, he would actually welcome the opportunity "to depart and be with Christ" (1:23), but for their sakes he would still want to remain on earth and strengthen them in faith. Paul's anchor is not his own strength or the power of his talents; it is Christ himself. We too hope to be able to say with him, "For me to live is Christ, and to die is gain"!

Part II: Exhortation to Unity

Statement of Principle (1:27-30). These verses contain the essence of Paul's message to the Philippians: that their manner of life be "worthy of the gospel of Christ" (1:27); and that they stand firm in faith as one community, courageous before their enemies while trusting in God's victory, even through their suffering for the sake of Christ.

First Example: Christ's Victory through Selflessness (2:1-18). Paul begins by reminding the Philippians that their life is "in Christ" and with fellowship "in the Spirit." This means kindness and compassion for one another, having the same attitude as Jesus, of whose body they are now members. Paul then inserts a hymn that dramatically illustrates what he means. This hymn, probably composed for a liturgical celebration, is an extraordinary witness to the growing understanding of Paul and the early Christian community of the preexistence of Christ before the Incarnation. Christ was "in the form of God," it says, but did not consider his status of being equal to God something to be selfishly held on to. Instead, he "emptied himself" to accept the condition of a slave, taking on the "likeness" of a human being, the "form" of a human, humble and obedient, even to death on a cross.

It must have been difficult for Paul and the early Christians to think of Jesus as divine, since Judaism was adamant that there was only one God, Yahweh. Jesus is not Yahweh, but nevertheless "equal" to him, his Son. He was "Son of God" before he became the son of Mary. Elsewhere, Paul states that "though Christ was rich [in heaven], he made himself poor for your sake, in order to make you rich by means of his poverty" (2 Corinthians 8:9), and ends that letter with a Trinitarian blessing: "The grace of the Lord Jesus Christ, the love of God [the Father], and the fellowship of the Holy Spirit be with you all" (2 Corinthians 13:13).

All the more striking, then, is Jesus' willingness to give all that up, become human, take on the condition of a "slave" (namely, sinful humanity), and suffer an ignominious death on the cross—all out of love for us and in obedience to the will of his Father. By way of reward, he was exalted on high as Lord of the whole universe, "to the glory of God the Father," that is, totally pleasing to the Father. It should be noted that the scene of Jesus' exaltation is modeled on the Old Testament exaltation of Yahweh according to Isaiah 45:23. Once again, a text that referred to Yahweh in the Old Testament is now applied to Jesus in the New.

The Philippians and we, fellow members of Christ's body, are not only asked to share his humility and obedient renunciation out of love for one another, but are also promised a share in his heavenly glory. Verses 12-18 urge us, therefore, to work out our salvation in "fear and trembling," that is, humbly cooperating with God. It is actually God who is "always at work" in us to bring about our salvation, so that we may shine as stars in the sky on the day of judgment, the Day of Christ!

Second Example: The Humble Service of Timothy and Epaphroditus (2:19-30). After such profound theology, Paul lightens the tone and promises to send to the Philippians his beloved companion Timothy as well as Epaphroditus, who had come in their name to care for Paul, but who had become so ill he almost died. Both these men were selfless and had the needs of the community at heart. Paul doubtlessly hoped that their presence in Philippi would help to bring peace.

Third Example: Paul Himself (3:1–4:1). Though writing from prison, Paul repeatedly breaks out in joy (Philippians 1:18; 2:17) and urges the Christian community to "rejoice in the Lord" with him (2:18; 3:1). The words "joy" or "rejoice" appear at least fifteen times in this letter! Why? Because Paul's heart was so taken with his new life in Christ that nothing else mattered by comparison. That is why he was so hard on those urging circumcision and keeping the proscriptions of

Judaism. Paul called them "dogs," "mutilators of the flesh." He himself had given up everything for the sake of Christ, including the hope he might have had of earning his salvation by being a "faultless" Jew and even Pharisee. He gave it all up, leaving his salvation totally in the hands of the Lord, trusting him in faith, love, and humility. He even accepted his own sufferings as a sharing in the death of Christ, with the hope that he would also "somehow" share in his resurrection. What an example for the Philippians to follow—pressing forward to win the prize for which God was calling him and all Christians: "heavenward in Christ Jesus" (3:14)!

Evodia and Syntyche (4:2-3). At this point, Paul addresses a dispute between two women in Philippi—Evodia and Syntyche, both of them "coworkers" in the gospel with Paul and another man named Clement. Was this simply a quarrel between two people, or was more at stake? Could both have been leaders of house churches in Philippi, and been at the source of a major rift in the community? In a homily on Philippians, St. John Chrysostom refers to the women as the *kephalaion* ("leadership") of the local church. Is this the climax of Paul's letter, the real issue underlying his varied appeals for humility and peace? Quite possibly! He asked them "to be of like mind" (Philippians 4:2), using the exact words of his call to the whole group in 2:2, as he introduced the wonderful example of Jesus' kenosis, self-emptying humility. It is a lesson for us too, that personal hurts left to fester could damage a whole community, while humble, compassionate interest in one another can heal.

Part III: Conclusion with Gratitude

Gospel Living (4:4-9). "Rejoice in the Lord always, again I say rejoice!" (4:4). Paul's summary of the Christian life begins with an expression of joy and a call to patience and prayer. The result promised is the peace of God which "surpasses all understanding." This peace can be maintained by thinking about "whatever is true, honorable, just, pure, lovely, gracious, excellent," as does Paul himself.

Final Exhortations (4:10-23). After thanking the Philippians for their kindness, Paul notes that he is at peace in whatever circumstances life may bring, pleasant or not. How? "I can do all things in him who strengthens me" (Philippians 4:13). So can we! In that vein, Paul promised that God "will supply every need of yours according to his riches in glory in Christ Jesus" (4:19). After sending greetings from his community, especially from "those of Caesar's household," Paul ends his letter with a beautiful prayer: "The grace of the Lord Jesus Christ be with your spirit." We still feel the power of this blessing today.

Philippians 1:1-11

1 Paul and Timothy, servants of Christ Jesus,
To all the saints in Christ Jesus who are in Philippi, with the bish-
ops and deacons:
2 Grace to you and peace from God our Father and the Lord
Jesus Christ.
3 I thank my God every time I remember you, 4 constantly praying with joy in every one of my prayers for all of you, 5 because of
your sharing in the gospel from the first day until now. 6 I am confident of this, that the one who began a good work among you will
bring it to completion by the day of Jesus Christ. 7 It is right for me
to think this way about all of you, because you hold me in your
heart, for all of you share in God's grace with me, both in my
imprisonment and in the defense and confirmation of the gospel.
8 For God is my witness, how I long for all of you with the compassion of Christ Jesus. 9 And this is my prayer, that your love may
overflow more and more with knowledge and full insight 10 to help
you to determine what is best, so that in the day of Christ you may
be pure and blameless, 11 having produced the harvest of righteousness that comes through Jesus Christ for the glory and praise of
God.

At the very beginning of his letter to the Philippians, Paul called his readers "saints" or "holy ones." But what makes someone a saint? When we hear the word, most of us think of the special Christians of the past—canonized saints—who are renowned because of their extraordinary holiness and witness, in some cases to the point of martyrdom. However, when Paul used the word "saint," he meant all Christians. That includes all of us!

In one sense, everyone who is baptized into Jesus' death and resurrection is a saint. This is not to diminish the special role of the canonized saints, but to highlight the immense gift that is for all of us in Christ. Because of the power of the cross, each Christian has the same inheritance in heaven as the great saints whose lives we commemorate in a special way.

Based on the characteristics that Paul mentioned in these few verses, we can begin to define what makes a person a "saint." Saints are "in Christ" (Philippians 1:1). United with Jesus, they all "share in God's grace" (1:7). They have access to the love and power of the Spirit in their everyday lives. Finally, because of "sharing in the gospel" (Philippians 1:5), they are all called and empowered to proclaim the gospel and advance the kingdom of God in the world. Baptized into Christ and filled with the Spirit, saints stand as a sign to the world of the love and power of God.

Do you believe that these characteristics are just as true of you as they were of the first believers? Like them, you too can be assured that God will bring to completion the "good work" he began in you at baptism (Philippians 1:6). The Holy Spirit will help you each day to take the steps that will enable you to embrace your full inheritance in Christ. Place your faith in Jesus. Believe that he is making you into a saint. Drink deeply of his grace and take possession of your inheritance. By God's grace, you can manifest his love to the world. You too can shine as one of God's holy ones.

"Father, thank you for giving me a share in the fellowship of your saints. By your Spirit, empower me to embrace Jesus and his life today."

Philippians 1:12-18

12 I want you to know, beloved, that what has happened to me
has actually helped to spread the gospel, 13 so that it has become
known throughout the whole imperial guard and to everyone else
that my imprisonment is for Christ; 14 and most of the brothers and
sisters, having been made confident in the Lord by my imprisonment, dare to speak the word with greater boldness and without
fear.
15 Some proclaim Christ from envy and rivalry, but others from
goodwill. 16 These proclaim Christ out of love, knowing that I have
been put here for the defense of the gospel; 17 the others proclaim
Christ out of selfish ambition, not sincerely but intending to
increase my suffering in my imprisonment. 18 What does it matter?
Just this, that Christ is proclaimed in every way, whether out of
false motives or true; and in that I rejoice.

Paul certainly was big-hearted and farsighted! Rather than complain about being in prison—as uncomfortable and unpleasant as it must have been—he assured the Philippians that God was bringing good from his adverse circumstances by using them to advance the gospel (Philippians 1:12-14). This assurance reflected his customary conviction and outlook on life that "all things work together for good for those who love God" (Romans 8:28).

Moreover, Paul wasn't worried about competitors or personal rivals who weren't sorry to see him in jail: He wasn't even disgruntled that some people were using his imprisonment as a chance to undercut him and gain a name for themselves by preaching the gospel (Philippians 1:15). Nor did he complain that others were promoting their own party's interests while he sat locked up (1:17). Instead, Paul simply rejoiced in the fact that Christ was being proclaimed, no matter what the motive (1:18).

Perhaps Paul had heard how Jesus himself once told his apostles, "Whoever is not against us is for us" (Mark 9:40) when they reprimanded an unknown, itinerant preacher who cast out demons in Jesus' name. Whatever the case, Paul didn't consider absolute purity of motives the highest requirement for Christian service. He recognized that all that really mattered was that the gospel be proclaimed, so that as many as possible could find salvation in Christ. All Paul had to do was look at his own background and past life to understand that God uses flawed and imperfect—even sinful—men and women to further his cause.

Competition, petty jealousies, ambition, and personal interests can permeate even of our best efforts at doing Christ's work. Attitudes like these can crop up in our own hearts and in just about every family, business, classroom, office, and parish that we know. Yet even with our weaknesses, failings, or less-than-perfect motives, we can still proclaim Christ and be his servants. So let's put aside any harsh criticisms or judgments against people who are serving the gospel. Let's focus instead on what is truly important: the common message we proclaim and the common life we share in Christ.

"Lord Jesus, give me the courage to speak your word no matter what situation I'm in. I want to proclaim your good news so that others can share in your salvation and know fullness of life in you."

Philippians 1:18-26

18 Yes, and I will continue to rejoice, 19 for I know that through
your prayers and the help of the Spirit of Jesus Christ this will turn
out for my deliverance. 20 It is my eager expectation and hope that I
will not be put to shame in any way, but that by my speaking with
all boldness, Christ will be exalted now as always in my body,
whether by life or by death. 21 For to me, living is Christ and dying
is gain. 22 If I am to live in the flesh, that means fruitful labor for
me; and I do not know which I prefer. 23 I am hard pressed between
the two: my desire is to depart and be with Christ, for that is far
better; 24 but to remain in the flesh is more necessary for you.
25 Since I am convinced of this, I know that I will remain and continue with all of you for your progress and joy in faith, 26 so that I
may share abundantly in your boasting in Christ Jesus when I come
to you again.

Shut beyond prison walls, with the shadow of a death sentence looming over him, Paul found the inner strength to exhort his beloved brothers and sisters in Philippi: "I will continue to rejoice, for I know that through your prayers and the help of the Spirit of Jesus Christ this will turn out for my deliverance" (Philippians 1:18-19).

Philippi hosted the first church Paul founded on the continent of Europe, and his writings exhibited a great personal fondness for the brothers and sisters there. He rejoiced at hearing of the community's continued faith and generosity as he encouraged them to remain united and joy-filled in the Lord.

Paul's warmth and enthusiasm are amazing, considering his imprisonment and impending trial, for his life was at stake! Yet his hope and trust in God were unfailing. "It is my eager expectation and hope that I will not be put to shame in any way, but that . . . Christ will be exalted now as always in my body, whether by life or by death" (Philippians 1:20). Despite his solitude and anguish, through prayer and faith Paul had come to understand that "living is Christ and dying is gain" (1:21).

Paul's faith is both a model and a challenge to us. We are called to fix our eyes on nothing so much as Jesus. Every day, we can ask him for a deeper awareness of his Spirit who dwells within us. We can turn to him often and utter short, simple prayers of love, faith, and trust. Every evening as we go to bed, we can ask the Lord to show us where we fell short during the day and to cleanse us with his blood. At Mass, we can fix our hearts on the sacrificial Lamb of God and worship and love him with all our mind, soul, and strength. It can be easy for circumstances to overwhelm our joy in the Lord. But is it really so hard to do such little things to accept Jesus' yoke? All he needs is a little bit of our hearts, and he can do wonders.

"Jesus, I surrender myself to you in this moment. I long to be in your presence more and more. Help me to remain steadfast in my faith."

Philippians 1:27-30

27 Only, live your life in a manner worthy of the gospel of Christ,
so that, whether I come and see you or am absent and hear about
you, I will know that you are standing firm in one spirit, striving
side by side with one mind for the faith of the gospel, 28 and are in
no way intimidated by your opponents. For them this is evidence of

their destruction, but of your salvation. And this is God's doing.
29 For he has graciously granted you the privilege not only of
believing in Christ, but of suffering for him as well— 30 since you
are having the same struggle that you saw I had and now hear that I
still have.

Stand firm in one spirit, striving side by side with one mind for the faith of the gospel. (Philippians 1:27)

One glimpse at any newspaper will show that many forces are at work against the gospel of Christ and those who live according to it. In Western society, we face temptations of materialism and greed. In large parts of the world, sexual immorality has become socially acceptable, even touted as an inherent human right. Abortion continues to threaten millions of unborn children a day, and euthanasia appears to be on the rise. Christians are regarded by many as naïve, backward, and uneducated. And sadly, Christian unity is undermined by divisions among Christians themselves.

The first-century Christians at Philippi faced opposition to the gospel as well. Paul realized that they were up against many challenges, even enemies. Nonetheless, he urged them to live in a manner "worthy of the gospel of Christ" (Philippians 1:27). Despite worldly pressures coming to bear on them and dangers threatening the community from rivalries within and opponents without, Paul encouraged them not to be frightened (1:28). Rather, they were to "stand firm in one spirit, striving side by side with one mind for the faith of the gospel" (1:27).

Paul understood that unity of mind and spirit can be a powerful source of protection and strength as well as a remedy against fear. When we are bonded together in love with fellow believers, whenever we seek to live together according to the gospel, we give witness to the world of the presence of God and of his ability and desire to bring salvation to all humanity.

To safeguard our faith against the deceptive ways of thinking and the sinful practices prevalent in contemporary society, it is "especially useful and very suited to our times that everyone should carefully study Christian doctrine, to the best of his ability, nourishing his mind with as much knowledge as possible of those truths that pertain to religion and can be grasped by human reason" (Pope Leo XIII, *On Christians as Citizens*, 17). So let us take seriously our responsibility to be well-instructed in our faith so that we will be able to live it without compromise, explain it when asked, and defend it if it is attacked. With the help of God's grace and the power of the Holy Spirit, may we stand firm and give witness to the gospel in the world today.

Philippians 2:1-4

1 If then there is any encouragement in Christ, any consolation
from love, any sharing in the Spirit, any compassion and sympathy,
2 make my joy complete: be of the same mind, having the same love,
being in full accord and of one mind. 3 Do nothing from selfish
ambition or conceit, but in humility regard others as better than
yourselves. 4 Let each of you look not to your own interests, but to
the interests of others.

St. Paul encouraged the Philippians to treat one another with Christlike humility and love. It's common to view humility as feeling bad about yourself or having a low opinion of yourself.

But the humility Paul wrote about is the kind that enables us to see ourselves and our neighbors as God sees us: as his beloved children and citizens of heaven. This kind of humility frees us to be like Jesus—to love unconditionally, to forgive, to forbear, and to share generously with those around us.

Humble people do not have to wear a mask or put on a show. Because they see other people's true value in God's eyes, they are not swayed by accidentals such as fame, wealth, or good looks. Humility puts others first, because it sees how important they are in God's eyes (Philippians 2:4).

Humility is a joy rather than a burden. It frees our hearts from fear and selfishness so that we can love our neighbor selflessly and generously. Pride, on the other hand, seeks to build our sense of importance by diminishing the value of others. Because it involves working hard to make us feel better than others, pride keeps us preoccupied with our own interests and cut off from the grace of God. It's humility that binds us together as the body of Christ.

Jesus is our model of humility. He humbled himself in order to free us from the burden of guilt and sin. His love excluded no one and made room for the least at his banquet table. He always welcomed the poor, the disabled, and the outcasts, and in him the humble found a close friend. Every day, God gives us opportunities to be like Jesus as we lovingly serve others in our homes and neighborhoods. When we share our blessings, both material and spiritual, with the needy around us, we experience love and blessing flowing from the throne of God. Our God is a God of infinite resources. We can be confident that whenever we take on his concerns and the needs of our neighbors, he will bless us and provide for all our needs.

"Lord Jesus, you humbled yourself for my sake. Free me from selfishness and pride so that I can become like you. Let me know the freedom of your love and find joy in seeking to serve rather than being served."

Philippians 2:5-11

5 Let the same mind be in you that was in Christ Jesus,
6 who, though he was in the form of God,
did not regard equality with God
as something to be exploited,
7 but emptied himself,
taking the form of a slave,
being born in human likeness.
And being found in human form,
8 he humbled himself
and became obedient to the point of death—
even death on a cross.

9 Therefore God also highly exalted him
and gave him the name
that is above every name,
10 so that at the name of Jesus
every knee should bend,
in heaven and on earth and under the earth,
11 and every tongue should confess
that Jesus Christ is Lord,
to the glory of God the Father.

Quoting from an early Christian hymn, St. Paul exhorted the Philippians to follow Jesus' example of humility. Though Jesus was the Son of God, he did not glory in his high position. Instead, he emptied himself and became like us (Philippians 2:6-7). He came "not to be served but to serve, and to give his life as a ransom for many" (Matthew 20:28). As Paul showed in this hymn, Jesus' death was but an extension of the way he lived his entire life: "Not my will but yours be done" (Luke 22:42).

Throughout his life, Jesus remained rooted in his Father's love and in his Father's will. In turn, we are now invited to root our lives completely in Jesus through faith and obedience. Each morning, we should ask ourselves: "Where will I be rooted today—in Christ, or in my own self? Where will I draw life from today—from Christ or from myself?" If we choose to root ourselves in Jesus, seeking our life from him, we have made the one decision that will make us victorious Christians.

Rooted in Christ, we are humble and needy. Rooted in self, we are prideful and self-sufficient. In Christ, we are freed to serve others. In self, we seek only to be served. In Christ, we will be obedient to God. In self, we will do whatever it takes to promote and preserve our lives. By rooting ourselves in Jesus, we can become pure vessels whom Jesus can use to pour out his life to all the world. Without Jesus, we are too full of ourselves to have any room for such grace.

Today, let us choose to be rooted in Jesus. Let us ask for the grace to become like him in his humility and love for all people. Let us have this mind of humility among ourselves. It is ours in Christ Jesus. By his life and death, Jesus has given us the perfect model of a humble and obedient child of God. Now he is raised up and highly exalted. Let us take on the name that is above all names, so that every tongue will confess that Jesus is Lord.

"Jesus, all glory to you! With all the angels and saints, I proclaim that you are Lord! Help me to root myself in you and draw my life from your rivers of living water."

Philippians 2:12-18

12 Therefore, my beloved, just as you have always obeyed me, not
only in my presence, but much more now in my absence, work out
your own salvation with fear and trembling; 13 for it is God who is
at work in you, enabling you both to will and to work for his good
pleasure.
14 Do all things without murmuring and arguing, 15 so that you
may be blameless and innocent, children of God without blemish in
the midst of a crooked and perverse generation, in which you shine
like stars in the world. 16 It is by your holding fast to the word of life
that I can boast on the day of Christ that I did not run in vain or
labor in vain. 17 But even if I am being poured out as a libation over
the sacrifice and the offering of your faith, I am glad and rejoice
with all of you— 18 and in the same way you also must be glad and
rejoice with me.

Do we ever stop and think of Paul's words, "God who is at work in you . . . for his good pleasure" (Philippians 2:13)? In the midst of getting through all the things that fill our lives each day, it's too easy to be oblivious to this reality!

But what if we did try to live this way—in Paul's phrase, "working out our salvation" (Philippians 2:12)—moment to moment? What if, to the best of our abilities, we followed his advice and did "all things without murmuring and arguing, so that you may be blameless and innocent, children of God without blemish" (2:14-15)? A life lived that way, even a little bit, can be such a witness. Consider the testimony of one person explaining why he was attracted to join a church youth group.

"You could see right away this group was different. They weren't abnormal, of course. They were a lot like the guys and girls I hung out with at school or on my team. Only, they didn't make fun of each other all the time, and they weren't trying to label people as losers or geeks.

"They weren't afraid to be themselves. At other parties I went to, all the people just stood around talking, not really doing anything, because they were afraid to act in some way that others would laugh at. But in this youth group, even the silliest activities were a lot of fun. Everyone got involved, whether it was charades on the spur of the moment, or a card game, or an intense volleyball game. I could see they enjoyed getting together.

"And whenever they prayed at the end of meetings, even that was fun. People really sang, I mean out loud, and they clapped their hands, and then shared about Jesus, too. It was the same stuff I learned about in religious education classes, only it was really happening in their lives. So, after coming to these Saturday night activities a few times, I was hooked. I wanted to be as happy and alive with Jesus as the kids I met there."

If we all try to "shine like stars in the world . . . holding fast to the word of life" (Philippians 2:15-16), we never know who may be watching—and being touched by God through us.

"O Christ our light, shine in my heart and burn brightly through my words and deeds today."

Philippians 2:19–3:1

19 I hope in the Lord Jesus to send Timothy to you soon, so that I
may be cheered by news of you. 20 I have no one like him who will
be genuinely concerned for your welfare. 21 All of them are seeking

their own interests, not those of Jesus Christ. 22 But Timothy's
worth you know, how like a son with a father he has served with
me in the work of the gospel. 23 I hope therefore to send him as
soon as I see how things go with me; 24 and I trust in the Lord that I
will also come soon.
25 Still, I think it necessary to send to you Epaphroditus—my
brother and co-worker and fellow soldier, your messenger and minister to my need; 26 for he has been longing for all of you, and has
been distressed because you heard that he was ill. 27 He was indeed
so ill that he nearly died. But God had mercy on him, and not only
on him but on me also, so that I would not have one sorrow after
another. 28 I am the more eager to send him, therefore, in order that
you may rejoice at seeing him again, and that I may be less anxious.
29 Welcome him then in the Lord with all joy, and honor such people, 30 because he came close to death for the work of Christ, risking
his life to make up for those services that you could not give me.
1 Finally, my brothers and sisters, rejoice in the Lord.
To write the same things to you is not troublesome to me, and
for you it is a safeguard.

What warm love and genuine affection for one another bound the early Christians together! The community in Philippi was especially dear to Paul because he had fathered its members in the faith. Far away in prison, he longed for news about the Philippians to cheer him up (Philippians 2:19). Moreover, moved with concern for them, he hoped to send Timothy to Philippi soon to encourage the believers there and help them resolve internal differences. "Like a son with a father," Timothy had served side by side with Paul in spreading the gospel. Now the apostle counted on his young friend's supportive presence nearby while he was in jail (1:20-23).

Paul's lines regarding Epaphroditus are further evidence of the care for each other that existed in the early church (Philippians 2:25-30). Paul's gratitude for the financial aid the Philippians sent him through Epaphroditus, his sorrow at Epaphroditus' grave illness, and his reassurances to the community in Philippi that their emissary was recovering well all reflect how deep the relationships were among the first-century believers.

In a world that tends to value self-reliance and independence over everything else, the witness of Christians loving and caring for one another can be a powerful testimony to the truth of the gospel. Healthy relationships and strong friendships in which we support one another are a source of stability, comfort, and encouragement in our lives: "Faithful friends are a sturdy shelter: whoever finds one has found a treasure. . . . Faithful friends are life-saving medicine; and those who fear the Lord will find them" (Sirach 6:14,16). As St. Aelred of Rievaulx, a twelfth-century Cistercian abbot and friend of St. Bernard of Clairvaux, wrote in his treatise *Spiritual Friendship*, "Friendship . . . heightens the joy of prosperity and mitigates the sorrows of adversity by dividing and sharing them. Hence, the best medicine in life is a friend."

Jesus has not called us to serve him in isolation but to join with fellow believers, united with one another in our efforts for the gospel. As we serve the Lord with other Christians, the Holy Spirit knits our hearts together. May we love and cherish all those Timothys and Epaphrodituses in our lives who have encouraged us and helped us grow as Christians: parents and family, teachers, friends, pastors, coworkers, fellow parishioners.

"Father, thank you for loving me and blessing me through the people whom you have sent into my life. Help me to support and encourage others through my love and friendship, too."

Philippians 3:2-11

2 Beware of the dogs, beware of the evil workers, beware of those
who mutilate the flesh! 3 For it is we who are the circumcision, who
worship in the Spirit of God and boast in Christ Jesus and have no
confidence in the flesh— 4 even though I, too, have reason for confidence in the flesh.

If anyone else has reason to be confident in the flesh, I have
more: 5 circumcised on the eighth day, a member of the people of
Israel, of the tribe of Benjamin, a Hebrew born of Hebrews; as to
the law, a Pharisee; 6 as to zeal, a persecutor of the church; as to
righteousness under the law, blameless.
7 Yet whatever gains I had, these I have come to regard as loss
because of Christ. 8 More than that, I regard everything as loss
because of the surpassing value of knowing Christ Jesus my Lord.
For his sake I have suffered the loss of all things, and I regard them
as rubbish, in order that I may gain Christ 9 and be found in him,
not having a righteousness of my own that comes from the law, but
one that comes through faith in Christ, the righteousness from
God based on faith. 10 I want to know Christ and the power of his
resurrection and the sharing of his sufferings by becoming like him
in his death, 11 if somehow I may attain the resurrection from the
dead.

Before meeting Jesus on the Damascus road, Paul's life was a model of Jewish moral and religious perfection. From the first days of his youth, he made every attempt to please God by conforming to the prescribed practices and laws of his people. Today, we might compare Paul's life before he met Christ to a man who was driven to fulfill all the right roles—choir boy, eagle scout, valedictorian of his graduating class, a successful businessman. Whether or not we have such a sterling record, it is typical of fallen humanity to look for our worth and value in our accomplishments, not in the love of the Lord.

When Paul met Jesus, however, he learned God's view about performance and acceptance—principally that our worth comes from the love of Christ Jesus, who gave his life for us. As a result of his encounter with Christ, Paul rejected his former way of life. Instead, his goal became to "gain Christ and be found in him, not having a righteousness of [his] own that comes from the law, but one that comes through faith in Christ" (Philippians 3:8-9). God accepts us as righteous because of the love he bears for us—a love he calls us to place our faith in. He does not measure our worth based on human standards of acceptance. Commenting on the centrality of Christ to our lives, Dietrich Bonhoeffer, a twentieth-century theologian and pastor, wrote:

> No other significance is possible, since Jesus is the only significance. Beside Jesus nothing has any significance. He alone matters. When we are called to follow Christ, we are summoned to an exclusive attachment to his person. The grace of his call bursts all the bonds of legalism. It is a gracious call, a gracious commandment. It transcends the difference between the law and the gospel. (*The Cost of Discipleship*)

Let us take time today to ponder the fact that God accepts us as righteous, not based on what we do, but based on our faith in Jesus. As our trust in God and our obedience to his word deepens, we too will be happy to proclaim: "Yet whatever gains I had, these I have come to regard as loss because of Christ. More than that, I regard everything as loss because of the surpassing value of knowing Christ Jesus my Lord" (Philippians 3:7-8).

Philippians 3:12-16

12 Not that I have already obtained this or have already reached
the goal; but I press on to make it my own, because Christ Jesus has
made me his own. 13 Beloved, I do not consider that I have made it
my own; but this one thing I do: forgetting what lies behind and
straining forward to what lies ahead, 14 I press on toward the goal for
the prize of the heavenly call of God in Christ Jesus. 15 Let those of us
then who are mature be of the same mind; and if you think differently about anything, this too God will reveal to you. 16 Only let us
hold fast to what we have attained.

Runners in a race focus all their energies and attention on crossing the finish line, their hopes fixed on winning the victory prize. Who knows? Perhaps Paul enjoyed cheering for the contestants competing in footraces in Greece, home of the ancient Olympics, or in similar competitions in his home of Tarsus. It's not unlikely, considering how Paul compared himself in his determination to attain union with God to an athlete running a race: "I press on toward the goal for the prize of the heavenly call of God in Christ Jesus" (Philippians 3:14).

Earlier in his life, Paul's energies had been directed toward obeying the Mosaic law. But after his conversion to Jesus—since "Christ Jesus has made me his own" (Philippians 3:12)—he redirected his energies to a higher goal. "Forgetting what lies behind and straining forward to what lies ahead" (3:13), he focused all his attention on gaining salvation and eternal life with Christ. Though he was living a good Christian life, Paul knew that he had not yet already "arrived," spiritually speaking. So he put forth his best efforts to cooperate with God's grace at work in him. Laying aside his reputation in Judaism and anything else that he had once considered important in order to find fulfillment in Christ, he urged the Philippians to do the same (3:15).

Using an analogy that reminds us of Paul's, St. Augustine wrote,

> Examine yourself. You should always be unhappy with what you are, if you want to attain what you are not yet. For when you were content with yourself, you stayed where you were, because if you say "Enough," you are finished that very minute. Always grow, always walk on, always advance; do not stop on the way, do not turn back, do not go off course. One who does not advance is standing still; one who returns to the things he already abandoned is going backwards. (*Sermon*, 169)

Similarly, St. John Chrysostom said,

> We should forget our successes, and throw them behind us. The runner reckons up not how many circuits he has finished, but how many are left. We too should reckon up, not how far we are advanced in virtue, but how much remains for us. . . . Thus the runner should run with great earnestness, with so great eagerness, without relaxation. (*Homily XII on the Philippians*)

Salvation is a gift from God—but it also demands our effort, just as a race demands every last ounce of a runner's strength. We are all runners still in the middle of the race, so let's not flag or sit down before we cross the finish line.

Philippians 3:17–4:1

17 Brothers and sisters, join in imitating me, and observe those who
live according to the example you have in us. 18 For many live as enemies of the cross of Christ; I have often told you of them, and now I
tell you even with tears. 19 Their end is destruction; their god is the
belly; and their glory is in their shame; their minds are set on earthly
things. 20 But our citizenship is in heaven, and it is from there that
we are expecting a Savior, the Lord Jesus Christ. 21 He will transform
the body of our humiliation that it may be conformed to the body of
his glory, by the power that also enables him to make all things subject to himself.
1 Therefore, my brothers and sisters, whom I love and long for,
my joy and crown, stand firm in the Lord in this way, my
beloved.

Among the faithful at Philippi were some whom Paul called "enemies of the cross of Christ," Christians whose lives were opposed to the cross. "Their god is the belly, and their glory is in their shame; their minds are set on earthly things" (Philippians 3:18,19). Paul directed the Philippians to the heavenlies and urged them to live as citizens of heaven.

How easily our minds become set on earthly things. Daily responsibilities and the lure of the good life quickly consume our thoughts and energy. The world, as well as our own flesh, repeatedly assures us that we "deserve a break." Nearly sixteen hundred years ago, St. John Chrysostom (*c.* 347-407) said: "Nothing is so incongruous in a Christian, and foreign to his character, as to seek ease and rest; and to be engrossed with present life is foreign to our profession and enlistment." Chrysostom was talking to people who "made a pretense of Christianity, yet live in ease and luxury . . . contrary to the cross. . . . For the cross belongs to a soul at its post for the fight, longing to die, seeking nothing else" (*Homilies on Philippians*, XIII).

We are enemies of the cross when our goals are fixed on this life, be it looking out for our own economic well-being without concern for society, striving to fulfill personal drives and pleasures regardless of the impact on others, or living for the moment contrary to the teachings of Scripture. John Chrysostom urged, rather: "Crucify yourself. . . . If you love the Master, die his death." This call is founded on great hope—our citizenship in heaven. Like Paul, we can count everything in our lives as loss (Philippians 3:8) because "our citizenship is in heaven" (3:20). Christ is there, interceding for us, our advocate before the throne of the Father (Romans 8:34).

Paul's hope was fixed on being with Jesus (Philippians 1:23), and it gave him tremendous joy. We can experience that hope too by befriending the cross. "Learn how great is the power of the cross, how many good things it has achieved, and does still; how it is the safety of our life" urged by John Chrysostom.

Our hope as Christians is found with Christ in the heavenlies. As we fix our eyes on Jesus, we will find the answer to all our desires. We will begin even now to know the power and love of God through Christ in a way that will bring life and hope to the world as we interact with those around us and respond to the suffering we see.

Philippians 4:2-3

2 I urge Euodia and I urge Syntyche to be of the same mind in
the Lord. 3 Yes, and I ask you also, my loyal companion, help these
women, for they have struggled beside me in the work of the
gospel, together with Clement and the rest of my co-workers,
whose names are in the book of life.

Paul's pleas in these two short verses took up only a line or two of space on the parchment roll, but they speak volumes about personal relationships among Christians. Love for one another and unity in the faith were marks of the believers of the first-century church, just as they are of Christians today. "We are one in the Spirit, we are one in the Lord," we sing, "and they'll know we are Christians by our love." Yet that love and unity is marred, at times, by our human failings, conflicts, and disagreements.

Earlier in his letter, Paul urged all the members of the community in Philippi to live in unity and love—to "stand firm in one spirit, striving side by side with one mind for the faith of the gospel" (Philippians 1:27). Now we find him pleading in particular with two dear friends of his to come to agreement with one another (4:2). Though Euodia and Syntyche had been zealous companions with Paul in the work of the gospel (4:3), that didn't make them "perfect" Christians. They were normal human beings, plagued by the weaknesses and sinful tendencies of their fallen human natures.

Clearly, these women had some kind of dispute with one another. But that didn't make Paul stop loving them or showing them respect. He was so deeply concerned about their well-being that he even asked other members of the church to help them work out their conflict (Philippians 4:3). Paul wasn't interested in the subject of the disagreement nor in judging who had been right or wrong. Instead, his main goal was that they restore their unity in the Lord.

Just as Paul had exhorted the Philippians to "be of the same mind, having the same love, being in full accord and of one mind" (Philippians 2:2), so might he exhort us today. Divisions among Christians grieve the heart of God and break the unity he desires for us. Disputes undermine our brotherly and sisterly relationships and our love for one another. Let's not allow conflicts, hurt feelings, or disagreements to interfere with our relationships or impair our effectiveness in the common cause of the gospel. Reconciliation is a Christian imperative: "So when you are offering your gift at the altar, if you remember that your brother or sister has something against you, leave your gift there before the altar and go; first be reconciled to your brother or sister, and then come and offer your gift" (Matthew 5:23-24).

"Father, I want to make 'every effort to maintain the unity of the Spirit in the bond of peace' (Ephesians 4:3). Help me to restore those relationships where I have allowed disagreement to separate me from others."

Philippians 4:4-9

4 Rejoice in the Lord always; again I will say, Rejoice. 5 Let your
gentleness be known to everyone. The Lord is near. 6 Do not worry
about anything, but in everything by prayer and supplication with
thanksgiving let your requests be made known to God. 7 And the
peace of God, which surpasses all understanding, will guard your
hearts and your minds in Christ Jesus.

8 Finally, beloved, whatever is true, whatever is honorable, whatever is just, whatever is pure, whatever is pleasing, whatever is
commendable, if there is any excellence and if there is anything
worthy of praise, think about these things. 9 Keep on doing the
things that you have learned and received and heard and seen in
me, and the God of peace will be with you.

Rejoice in the Lord always. . . . Do not worry about anything.
(Philippians 4:4,6)

Paul's words ring with the confidence and conviction that God was in charge of his life—and of the lives of his dear friends in Philippi. He experienced the joy and peace that come from being securely rooted in the Lord, and he knew that his brothers and sisters in Christ could have that same experience, too.

The testimony of Paul's own life backed up his encouragement to the Philippians to rejoice and not be anxious about anything at all. Even as he sat in prison, Paul remained joyful. That's because his joy was not dependent on his circumstances, but on his knowledge of Christ Jesus and Christ's unfailing love for him. Even faced with the threat of death, he was at peace because his trust was in the God who promises eternal life to those who believe. Because his own witness from his prison cell was credible, Paul could urge the church in Philippi to follow his example and exhortations: "Keep on doing the things that you have learned and received and heard and seen in me" (Philippians 4:9).

Paul's prison witness has been repeated countless times over through the centuries. While in the Tower of London awaiting his execution in 1535, St. Thomas More wrote: "I trust Christ will place his holy hand on me and in the stormy seas hold me up from drowning." Similarly, while imprisoned in a bamboo cage in nineteenth-century

Vietnam, St. Theophane Venard remained joyful and encouraged his family in a letter he wrote them to have the same approach:

> From day to day I expect my sentence. Perhaps tomorrow I shall be led to execution. . . . Only a few short hours, and my soul will quit this earth, will finish her exile, will have done with the fight. I shall mount upwards and reach our own true home. . . . Adieu, dearest father, sister, brothers, do not mourn for me, do not weep for me. . . . Practice your religion; keep pure from all sin. We shall meet again in heaven, and shall enjoy true happiness in the kingdom of God.

We are not likely to face imprisonment and martyrdom like Paul, Thomas More, and Theophane Venard. Still, in the challenges and trials we encounter each day, the "peace of God, which surpasses all understanding," can keep our hearts and minds in Christ Jesus (Philippians 4:7). Because of our assurance of the Lord's care and love for us, we can be free from crippling anxiety and fear. Because it is the Lord in whom we rejoice and not what is happening around us, our joy can be steady and constant.

Philippians 4:10-23

[10] I rejoice in the Lord greatly that now at last you have revived
your concern for me; indeed, you were concerned for me, but had
no opportunity to show it. [11] Not that I am referring to being in
need; for I have learned to be content with whatever I have. [12] I
know what it is to have little, and I know what it is to have plenty.

In any and all circumstances I have learned the secret of being
well-fed and of going hungry, of having plenty and of being in
need. 13 I can do all things through him who strengthens me.
14 In any case, it was kind of you to share my distress.
15 You Philippians indeed know that in the early days of the
gospel, when I left Macedonia, no church shared with me in the
matter of giving and receiving, except you alone. 16 For even when
I was in Thessalonica, you sent me help for my needs more than
once. 17 Not that I seek the gift, but I seek the profit that accumu-
lates to your account. 18 I have been paid in full and have more
than enough; I am fully satisfied, now that I have received from
Epaphroditus the gifts you sent, a fragrant offering, a sacrifice
acceptable and pleasing to God. 19 And my God will fully satisfy
every need of yours according to his riches in glory in Christ Jesus.
20 To our God and Father be glory forever and ever. Amen.
21 Greet every saint in Christ Jesus. The friends who are with me
greet you. 22 All the saints greet you, especially those of the
emperor's household.
23 The grace of the Lord Jesus Christ be with your spirit.

One way to read Paul's letter to the Philippians is as one long thank-you note for their generous support and encouragement during his time of suffering and imprisonment. He called their charity "a fragrant offering, a sacrifice acceptable and pleasing to God" (Philippians 4:18).

What motivated the Philippians' generosity? A grateful heart for sure! They were grateful for the gospel they received through Paul's ministry, and they rejoiced in the opportunity to express their gratitude. "God loves a cheerful giver" (2 Corinthians 9:7). Whenever we make a contribution to the work of the Lord in church or give money in support of the poor, God looks on it as a gift to himself as well. That is why Jesus told his disciples, "As you did it to one of the least of these who are members of my family, you did it to me" (Matthew 25:40).

What we have to offer may look very small to us and not worth much, but it is not insignificant to God. Jesus praised a poor widow who put two pennies into the collection basket in the Temple (Luke 21:1-4). He remarked that she gave more than the rich because her gift came from her poverty. This poor widow gave all she had.

St. Luke, a close friend of Paul's, tells of another generous woman, Tabitha, who was noted for her "good works and acts of charity" (Acts 9:36). After her death, all the widows of Joppa assembled to testify before Peter to the kindness she had shown them. It sounds like she too was a giver with a grateful and generous heart. The point is that any gift given out of love is invaluable. The amount or size doesn't matter as much as the cost to the giver.

Jesus promised that the measure we give will be the measure we receive (Mark 4:24). We can never outdo God in giving! He gives the treasures of his kingdom beyond measure: peace, joy, and righteousness in this life and the promise of seeing him face to face in his everlasting kingdom.

"Lord Jesus, widen our hearts to share freely the gifts you have given us, so that all who suffer want, especially the poor, the homeless, and the jobless, may find everything they need."

A Panoramic View of the Church and Every Believer

THE LETTER TO THE COLOSSIANS

An Introduction to the Letter to the Colossians

by Fr. George Montague, S.M.

At the base of Mount Cadmus in Turkey's Lycus river valley lie the ruins of a city destroyed by earthquake but made famous by the letter you are about to read. Colossae lay about 120 miles east of the port city Ephesus in Asia Minor. With its neighboring cities Hierapolis and Laodicea, it formed a sort of triangle along the Lycus River, and all three profited by their location along or near the major trade route from Ephesus on the west coast to the towns of Iconium and Tarsus in the southeast.

Famous for its purple-colored wool, Colossae had, along with its sister cities, a respectable Jewish population by Paul's time, and no doubt it was among them that a disciple of Paul, probably Epaphras, evangelized and founded the first Christian community. The fact that it was a disciple rather than the apostle himself who began the community there attests to the vitality of Paul's ministry during his three-year stay in Ephesus (A.D. 54-57), when "a wide door for effective work has opened to me" (1 Corinthians 16:9) and "all the residents of Asia . . . heard the word of the Lord" (Acts 19:10). Colossae was the home of Philemon and his runaway slave Onesimus, as well as Apphia and Archippus (Philemon 2), the latter a minister in the church (Colossians 4:17).

We know that the letters of Paul were shared beyond the communities for which he wrote, but this is expressly requested in this letter. He asks that the letter be read also in Laodicea and that the one to the

Laodiceans be read to the church in Colossae (Colossians 4:16). Since Epaphras also worked in Hierapolis and Laodicea, we can assume that the letters would be read there as well. The New Testament does not tell us anything about the Laodicean letter. It has been suggested that it was the Letter to the Ephesians, but this is conjecture. What is significant for us is that the word of God addressed to one church in its particular circumstances is applicable to another. Granted that adjustments have to be made according to differing circumstances, this is still what is going on in the church today. Letters addressed to churches of two millennia ago are read in our churches as messages to us. And even in the privacy of our homes or in study groups, we can read them and study them as God's word *now*.

By Paul or a Disciple? Scholars today are divided on the question of whether this letter was actually written by Paul or by a disciple, either in his lifetime or later. In ancient times, the word *author* meant the *authority* behind a writing, not necessarily the one who actually wrote the letter. Most letters in the ancient world, at least official ones, were dictated to scribes who specialized in putting the author's words on papyrus or parchment. Even today in largely oral cultures like India, one can see "scribes" sitting in the street with a typewriter and passers-by stopping to dictate a letter—for a fee, of course. Paul certainly dictated in this fashion, as we know from those letters in which he calls attention to the fact that he is writing the conclusion to the letter in his own hand ("with what large letters," Galatians 6:11; 1 Corinthians 16:21; 2 Thessalonians 3:17; Philemon 19). He does so also in the Letter to the Colossians (4:18).

Could Paul even assign one of his disciples to write in his name? We know that presidents have speechwriters, who craft the author's ideas in good rhetorical style, and whose final draft is approved and used by the speaker as his own. Why not Paul? If he spent nearly half his ministry in prison, at times in dire conditions, this alternative of a "ghostwriter" seems likely. 1 Peter 5:12 speaks explicitly of using Silvanus (a disciple of Paul) in composing that letter.

Many scholars, however, think that this process continued after Paul's death, namely that some of the letters attributed to Paul were written by early disciples to apply the teaching of Paul to a later situation. Among the reasons offered for this alternative in the case of Colossians are the following: (1) *Words used*: There are eighty-seven words in Colossians that do not appear in the letters everyone agrees were written by Paul. (2) The *style* of writing is very different from the other letters of Paul: long, hymnic-like sentences. (3) The *theology* of Colossians is more developed than in the earlier letters of Paul: Christ's preexistence and role in creation; "church" as a universal body rather than the local community; Christ is now the *head* of his body. (4) "Realized eschatology," that is, the author has moved the future glory into the present; for example, by baptism we are already raised with Christ (2:12; 3:1). (5) The false teaching Paul addresses fits better at a later time.

Some of these arguments, however, are very weak. The difference of vocabulary can easily be explained by a difference of subject matter. If in writing a letter today we had to limit ourselves to the words or ideas we used in a letter five years ago, how could we possibly talk about a new subject matter? Scholars sometime use arguments that contradict one another. If some claim that difference of vocabulary points to a different author, one highly respected Pauline scholar holds that Paul didn't write Colossians because some passages in it are almost verbatim to those found in 1 Thessalonians, 1 Corinthians, and Philippians! One author says differences prove pseudonymity; another says the similarities do.

The particular *style* might have been chosen to fit the lyrical, liturgical style treasured by the Colossians, particularly if the scribe was Epaphras, who knew the Colossians well, having evangelized them. As for developed theology, why should Paul be confined to the thought he expressed in his earlier letters, particularly since the developments can also be shown to be in continuity with his earlier statements? For example, that Christ should be the head of all creation is stated in 1 Corinthians 8:6: "For us there is . . . one Lord Jesus Christ through whom are all things and through whom exist."

And as for "realized eschatology," what of Paul's statement in Romans that we have already been glorified (8:30) that stands alongside his statement that we will be glorified (8:17)—just as in Colossians we have both the already ("you were raised with him," Colossians 2:12) and the not yet ("Christ in you, your hope for glory," 1:27)? Then there are the persons mentioned in the letter. Of the ten people mentioned in the brief letter to Philemon, eight are mentioned in Colossians. If it were a later writer sending this letter to Philemon's home community, would not the recipients have known that the names came from a different time?

As in many questions about historical issues, we have only the "certitude of probabilities." But let us imagine that indeed a later author in the school of Paul saw a deteriorating situation in one of Paul's communities, Colossae. He responded with a letter that applies, with appropriate developments, what Paul would have said to this situation. Knowing Paul's thoughts well, he would want them to know that he is speaking with Paul's authority. Thus, even in this situation (which has many weaknesses, as shown previously), it would be the continuing voice of Paul addressing a situation he had not foreseen in his lifetime. We see here the *apostolic tradition*, which the church judged to be authentic when it incorporated Colossians into the canon of inspired Scriptures.

The Message. The question of authorship, therefore, need not distract us from the message the letter had for the Colossians then and the message it has for us today. For the sake of simplicity, however, in what follows Paul is assumed to be the author.

(1) *Christ, the Head of All That Is.* In a beautiful hymn near the very beginning of the letter, Paul plays on the idea of the "firstborn," a term that would have deep meaning for the Jewish members of the community. The firstborn was the heir, the successor to his father in the household, with authority over his younger brothers. Christ is the "firstborn of creation," which, in the line that follows, really means "born before all creation," since "all things were created in him and through him and for him" (Colossians 1:15-16). Among "all things," Paul gives special place to the angels, for Christ is above them—a point Paul hopes will not be lost on the Colossians, who have become excessive in their estimation of angels (see below). But Christ is also the "firstborn from the dead," because through his resurrection God has shown him to be the highest of all beings, the head of his body, which is the church. He was not only *in* the beginning; he *is* the beginning (1:18), both of creation and of the new creation begun with his resurrection.

(2) *Christ above the Angels.* The Colossians have been infected, it seems, with a view of the angels that has diminished Christ. How could this be? The angels are pure spirits, and even they are in a hierarchy. Christ, however, is human flesh, and so he must be lower than the angels. Paul counters this in several ways, and first of all in the hymn that places him above "things visible and invisible, whether thrones or domina-

tions, or principalities or powers," which are the angelic choirs (Colossians 1:16). In our day we have seen an explosion of interest in angels, even in popular television programs. Angels play an important role in the Bible—chief among them Raphael, the angel of healing, Gabriel, the announcer of the good news, and Michael, the victor over Lucifer. And Jesus speaks of the guardian angels who "always behold the face of my heavenly Father" (Matthew 18:10). But Christ was involved even in the creation of the angels, and all the "fullness of the divinity" dwells in him bodily (Colossians 2:9). The humanity of Jesus is therefore even above the angels, because it is the humanity of the Son of God! For this reason, it is important today not to allow enthusiasm about the angels to lead us to forget that they are only servants of the King of kings and Lord of lords.

The Church, the Body of Christ. When Paul says that "in him dwells the fullness of the godhead bodily," he immediately adds, "and you share in this fullness in him, who is the head of every principality and power" (Colossians 2:10). That means that in Christ we share in his supremacy over the angels! The church is above the angels! Why? Because the church is his body, and that is a privilege the angels do not have. It is part of the "scandal" of the Incarnation that God would bypass the angels to become a man. And more: The great work of Christ did not redeem the angels. The cross and the resurrection reconciled the lost human race to God (1:20). It defeated the powers and principalities that held the race subject. And, as in Ephesians 2:14-18, the formation of the church is cosmic peacemaking, establishing all creation in a right relation to God. Now the church carries on the battle for such peace (6:15).

Constant Growth. Paul is writing to Christians who are already "in Christ." At times he is so optimistic about their salvation that it seems they are already in heaven (Colossians 3:3). Yet he realizes that they are still on a journey, a life in the "not yet." For this reason at the beginning of the letter, he prays for their spiritual growth. He prays first for their advance in "knowledge of his will through all spiritual wisdom and understanding." No doubt he is asking that they be disposed to accept Paul's teaching about the primacy of Christ. But this is not just a matter of Paul laying out the right doctrine. They must be interiorly taught by the Holy Spirit, or all the external teaching will do no good. Enlightenment is thus a gift of God, and only in the atmosphere of humble prayer can it be received. The effect of this enlightenment is that they may "live in a manner worthy of the Lord," and that means good works, endurance, patience, joy, and thanksgiving (1:10-12). This prayerful introduction prepares for the moral exhortations that follow in chapter 3, with applications to the Christian family, slaves, and masters.

A Letter with a Large Vision. For us, the Letter to the Colossians is a call to think big—to think cosmically, for all creation belongs to Christ. His redemptive act puts all creation back on track for the glory of God. This does not permit passivity on our part but rather a faith-filled cooperation in completing what Christ has done. It is through the church that the kingdom will come. And our cooperation may not only be good works but suffering the cross as Paul did, with the assurance that like him, we can fill up in our "flesh what is lacking to the sufferings of Christ for his body, the church" (Colossians 1:24). Though Christ's redemptive act is infinitely meritorious, having no need for our help, it is part of his goodness that he lets us share in bringing about the kingdom. Colossians gives us a magnificent blueprint for doing so.

Colossians 1:1-8

1 Paul, an apostle of Christ Jesus by the will of God, and Timothy
our brother,
2 To the saints and faithful brothers and sisters in Christ in
Colossae: Grace to you and peace from God our Father.
3 In our prayers for you we always thank God, the Father of our Lord
Jesus Christ, 4 for we have heard of your faith in Christ Jesus and of
the love that you have for all the saints, 5 because of the hope laid up
for you in heaven. You have heard of this hope before in the word of
the truth, the gospel 6 that has come to you. Just as it is bearing fruit
and growing in the whole world, so it has been bearing fruit among
yourselves from the day you heard it and truly comprehended the grace
of God. 7 This you learned from Epaphras, our beloved fellow servant.
He is a faithful minister of Christ on your behalf, 8 and he has made
known to us your love in the Spirit.

How thankful Paul must have been! What he himself had experienced was happening all over the world. People were coming to know that God grants life, purpose, forgiveness, and joy through Jesus. Through Christ, men and women in Colossae had received the Spirit and were living with a knowledge of God's will and an assurance of his love.

As he opened his letter to the Colossians, Paul mentioned the one who had introduced them to Jesus: a layman named Epaphras (Colossians 1:7-8). Evidently, Epaphras had gone to Colossae to pass on to others what he had come to learn—that Jesus is the wisdom of God, the One through whom everything exists and the One through whom everything is reconciled to God (1:15-20). The Colossians who believed Epaphras's message now joined him in looking forward to eternal life with Christ. Day by day, they were able to bear the fruit of their new lives (1:4-7).

We too can rejoice that the gospel has been preached to us. Each in our own way, we can do what Epaphras did. We all can make Christ known.

Sometimes, the fear of "not doing it right" or of "sounding too preachy" might cause us to leave this mission to professionals like priests and religious. But who will convey the gospel in our homes, our neighborhoods, or our workplaces if we don't? God wants each of us to be confident that he has given us a share in his saving work in the world. The Spirit is with us to guide and strengthen us. He can make use of all our efforts to share the gospel—however small or halting they may be—and teach us as we go along. We need only keep our hearts open to Jesus. This will fill us with a desire to witness and keep us searching for more and more creative ways to communicate the gospel.

"Holy Spirit, fill me with the desire that Jesus would reign in the hearts of all people. Thank you for the joy of his presence in me. Guide me in helping others to come to know him, too."

Colossians 1:9-14

9 For this reason, since the day we heard it, we have not ceased
praying for you and asking that you may be filled with the knowledge of God's will in all spiritual wisdom and understanding, 10 so
that you may lead lives worthy of the Lord, fully pleasing to him, as
you bear fruit in every good work and as you grow in the knowledge

of God. 11 May you be made strong with all the strength that comes
from his glorious power, and may you be prepared to endure everything with patience, while joyfully 12 giving thanks to the Father,
who has enabled you to share in the inheritance of the saints in the
light. 13 He has rescued us from the power of darkness and transferred us into the kingdom of his beloved Son, 14 in whom we have
redemption, the forgiveness of sins.

Everyone who wants to follow Jesus knows how important it is to pray. But do we know why? St. Paul's words to the Colossians give us one vital reason. It is in prayer that we can receive the knowledge of God's will, be filled with spiritual wisdom and understanding, and be empowered to lead lives worthy of the Lord (Colossians 1:9-11). It is in prayer, as we come face-to-face with the Father who loves us and the Lamb of God who died for us, that our hearts and minds are transformed. It is in prayer that we can know the comfort of the Spirit as we face the challenges of living in this world.

Throughout his life, Jesus' wisdom, compassion, humility, and unconditional love were a constant testimony to the importance of prayer. Prayer was so vital a part of Jesus' life that we might say that his miracles and sermons were those things he did in the moments between his times of prayer. So, when we fix our eyes on Jesus, we can get a glimpse of who we can become as we pray: not just servants of the gospel; not just children of God; but *partakers in the divine nature* as well.

Do you need godly wisdom for your life? Family? Work? Future? Do you find it hard to understand what your "next step" should be? Scripture promises, "If any of you is lacking in wisdom, ask God, who gives to all generously and ungrudgingly, and it will be given you" (James 1:5). Just as Jesus provided an abundance of wine at the wedding of Cana, he longs to pour an abundance of wisdom into the heart of the person who prays. Let us be reachable and open, and ask for this most precious gift.

With Jesus as our model and our focus, let us daily flee to a place of solitude, silence, and prayer within our hearts, where God resides. As we do, God will pour his wisdom into us. We will be filled with the knowledge of his will and equipped to live a life worthy of him.

"Heavenly Father, take me by the hand and lead me into the solitude of prayer. Let me experience your transforming power. You are the all-wise God. Put your wisdom and understanding into my open heart. May I become like Jesus, equipped for every good work."

Colossians 1:15-20

15 He is the image of the invisible God, the firstborn of all creation; 16 for in him all things in heaven and on earth were created,
things visible and invisible, whether thrones or dominions or rulers
or powers—all things have been created through him and for him.
17 He himself is before all things, and in him all things hold
together. 18 He is the head of the body, the church; he is the beginning, the firstborn from the dead, so that he might come to have
first place in everything. 19 For in him all the fullness of God was
pleased to dwell, 20 and through him God was pleased to reconcile
to himself all things, whether on earth or in heaven, by making
peace through the blood of his cross.

How can Paul's words about Jesus do anything but inspire us with awe and wonder? Jesus Christ, the eternal Son of God, is the firstborn of all creation. Everything in heaven and on earth was made for him. He alone is the perfect image of the invisible God, and nothing in the whole of creation can compare with him.

Paul didn't write these things about Jesus to portray him as a distant, unapproachable deity who has no interest in us mere mortals. No, Paul spoke of Jesus' grandeur in order to give us a sense of security concerning the life we have inherited in him. If Jesus is truly the one in whom God's fullness is pleased to dwell, then without a doubt he is able to give us "the inheritance of the saints in the light" (Colossians 1:12). The more we come to know Jesus as the holy and powerful Son of God, the more confident and peaceful we will become in every situation we face.

What do you see when you envision Jesus? Do you imagine the eternal Son of God, filled with all power and authority, making a way through death into life for you? Do you see the one through whom all things were created offering himself to the Father because of his covenant with you? Everything holds together in Jesus. He is ever faithful to his promises, and he will not abandon you in your hour of need.

Perhaps a loved one is seriously ill or has died. Run to Jesus, knowing that he holds you and your loved one in the palm of his hand. He who is the firstborn from the dead will give you the strength and peace you need. Perhaps you face a difficult relationship with a relative or coworker. Allow Jesus, through whom God has reconciled all things to himself, to guide you in repentance and reconciliation. If you feel alone or distant from God, reach out to Jesus. Remember that God has given you peace through the blood of his cross. He will answer you!

"Glory to you, Son of God, Lord Jesus Christ! I worship you for your immense power and glory, but I also rejoice in your intimate love. What more is there for me to do but to kneel at your feet in adoration?"

Colossians 1:21-23

21 And you who were once estranged and hostile in mind, doing
evil deeds, 22 he has now reconciled in his fleshly body through
death, so as to present you holy and blameless and irreproachable
before him— 23 provided that you continue securely established
and steadfast in the faith, without shifting from the hope promised
by the gospel that you heard, which has been proclaimed to every
creature under heaven. I, Paul, became a servant of this gospel.

Our heavenly Father prepared a perfect plan for showering each of us with his life, his peace, and his presence. How the Father's heart must have broken when our first parents—and every subsequent generation—chose to turn away and reject all he had in store for them! Although God's holiness could not allow us in our sinfulness to stay in his presence, in his relentless love, our Father could not let us go. This is why he chose to restore us to himself through the obedience and sacrifice of his Son on the cross.

Perhaps we find it hard to admit that we were hostile in our hearts and minds toward God (Colossians 1:21). But this is exactly where Jesus found us when he became man and reached out to save us. And, to a certain extent, this is how he finds us every day. We continue to need his forgiveness throughout our lives, as we struggle with anger toward others, fear, lustful thoughts, hopelessness, and a host of other sins. The more we allow the Holy Spirit to show us how deeply we need Jesus, the more we will be able to receive the healing, cleansing, and freedom that he won for us on the cross.

Let us ask God to show us where we need his forgiveness and grace to change. Jesus longs to plant his cross right in the midst of all our struggles and weaknesses so that the Holy Spirit can reveal the power of the cross to free us. Jesus can enter any situation and protect and deliver us. We can proclaim the authority of Jesus' cross whenever Satan tries to tempt us or lead us to believe things that are not true.

Today in prayer, fix your gaze on the cross and let Jesus tell you, "You are loved beyond measure!" Through his death he has reconciled you to God and wants to present you "holy and blameless and irreproachable" before the Father (Colossians 1:22)! Allow the Lord to take you closer to himself through his cross.

"Father, I was lost and without hope. But you have raised me from darkness. You have cleared away the shame of sin. You have embraced me. I am so grateful to you! May Jesus' cross stand at the center of my life."

Colossians 1:24–2:5

24 I am now rejoicing in my sufferings for your sake, and in my
flesh I am completing what is lacking in Christ's afflictions for the
sake of his body, that is, the church. 25 I became its servant according to God's commission that was given to me for you, to make the
word of God fully known, 26 the mystery that has been hidden
throughout the ages and generations but has now been revealed to
his saints. 27 To them God chose to make known how great among
the Gentiles are the riches of the glory of this mystery, which is
Christ in you, the hope of glory. 28 It is he whom we proclaim,
warning everyone and teaching everyone in all wisdom, so that we

may present everyone mature in Christ. 29 For this I toil and struggle with all the energy that he powerfully inspires within me.
1 For I want you to know how much I am struggling for you, and
for those in Laodicea, and for all who have not seen me face to
face. 2 I want their hearts to be encouraged and united in love, so
that they may have all the riches of assured understanding and
have the knowledge of God's mystery, that is, Christ himself, 3 in
whom are hidden all the treasures of wisdom and knowledge. 4 I am
saying this so that no one may deceive you with plausible arguments. 5 For though I am absent in body, yet I am with you in spirit,
and I rejoice to see your morale and the firmness of your faith in
Christ.

It was a common practice in the early church to borrow words from the surrounding culture and consecrate them for a specific Christian use. For example, the word "baptism" comes from an everyday word for immersing and washing. Another such word which was consecrated is "mystery," which appears twenty-eight times in the New Testament (mostly in Pauline writings), including three times in this passage (Colossians 1:26,27; 2:2).

Our English word "mystery" comes from the Greek *mysterion*, but over the centuries it has acquired many new layers of meaning by secular usage. Today the word tends to evoke images of something shadowy or unknowable, perhaps even sinister. One cannot always assume, however, that the popular connotation of a term corresponds to the biblical meaning.

Paul's mission was to "make the word of God fully known, the *mystery* that has been hidden throughout the ages and generations but has now been revealed to his saints" (Colossians 1:25-26). For Paul and those of his tradition, the mystery was the content of the revelation given by God; it focuses on his eternal purposes.

The mystery is the plan of God hidden in himself before the creation of the world. The revelation of this plan takes place in the passage of time—being worked out in historical events. The fullness of God's plan is revealed in the incarnation of his Son. Jesus took on a body, lived in history, and through his death and resurrection revealed God's plan of salvation. He is himself the embodiment of the mystery—the revelation and working out of God's eternal plan.

When the gospel is preached, it does more than just impart some new ideas. It makes present in power the reality of the death and resurrection of Jesus. The church, the body of Christ, really lives and suffers in history just as Christ really lived and suffered in history. It is through the church acting in history that God completes the revelation of his plan to all creation.

In the same way, our personal decisions affect the manner in which salvation history continues to unfold. Our participation in the mystery, the working out of God's plan, is the foundation that gives meaning to our lives. Therefore, we can see the importance of our decision to pray daily, to participate in the life of the church, and to serve the Lord and his people.

"Lord, make me a part of your plan."

Colossians 2:6-15

6 As you therefore have received Christ Jesus the Lord, continue
to live your lives in him, 7 rooted and built up in him and established in the faith, just as you were taught, abounding in thanksgiving.
8 See to it that no one takes you captive through philosophy and
empty deceit, according to human tradition, according to the elemental spirits of the universe, and not according to Christ. 9 For in
him the whole fullness of deity dwells bodily, 10 and you have come
to fullness in him, who is the head of every ruler and authority.
11 In him also you were circumcised with a spiritual circumcision,
by putting off the body of the flesh in the circumcision of Christ;
12 when you were buried with him in baptism, you were also raised
with him through faith in the power of God, who raised him from
the dead. 13 And when you were dead in trespasses and the uncircumcision of your flesh, God made you alive together with him,
when he forgave us all our trespasses, 14 erasing the record that
stood against us with its legal demands. He set this aside, nailing it
to the cross. 15 He disarmed the rulers and authorities and made a
public example of them, triumphing over them in it.

What a marvel St. Paul was! In letter after letter, he revealed an all-consuming love for Jesus, even as he wrote the most profound theology. No wonder he is often referred to simply as "the Apostle." No other title is necessary. Bearing all this in mind, we might be tempted to conclude that we could never attain Paul's level of holiness. After all, we're just weak, ordinary people who are extremely busy with the everyday demands of life. The pace of our lives is so much faster than Paul's. We all have so many duties and obligations.

But Paul was a busy man himself. In addition to having to earn his living as a tent maker, he made at least three missionary trips—each one stretching hundreds of miles—through modern-day Syria, Turkey, Greece, and beyond. He founded churches wherever he went, maintained a very involved correspondence, and was an effective fundraiser for the struggling church in Jerusalem. And, all this work was constantly being interrupted by illness, persecution, imprisonment, even shipwreck. Yet Paul still found time to turn to the Lord in prayer. If he can do it, so can we!

Our ordinariness or busyness does not have to limit us to a life of spiritual poverty. The answer lies in devoting the time and energy we do have to learning who we are in Christ. Do we trust that in baptism we "have come to fullness in him" (Colossians 2:10)? Do we understand that we are buried with Christ, so that we have been released from the regime of sin? Have we begun to experience a loving relationship with the Father?

Every day, Jesus calls us to receive life in his presence. He is always ready to open our eyes to what he has accomplished in us through baptism and to show us how he wants to move in us today. Every one of us can become living signs of reconciliation with God—just as Paul was. Let us make the most of every opportunity to increase our knowledge of him so that we may become a channel of his blessing to others.

"Lord Jesus, I want to be open to you and your teaching today. Teach me to be bold in my faith and to spread your kingdom in the power of the Holy Spirit."

Colossians 2:16-23

16 Therefore do not let anyone condemn you in matters of food
and drink or of observing festivals, new moons, or sabbaths.
17 These are only a shadow of what is to come, but the substance
belongs to Christ. 18 Do not let anyone disqualify you, insisting on
self-abasement and worship of angels, dwelling on visions, puffed
up without cause by a human way of thinking, 19 and not holding
fast to the head, from whom the whole body, nourished and held
together by its ligaments and sinews, grows with a growth that is
from God.
20 If with Christ you died to the elemental spirits of the universe,
why do you live as if you still belonged to the world? Why do you
submit to regulations, 21 "Do not handle, Do not taste, Do not
touch"? 22 All these regulations refer to things that perish with use;
they are simply human commands and teachings. 23 These have
indeed an appearance of wisdom in promoting self-imposed piety,
humility, and severe treatment of the body, but they are of no value
in checking self-indulgence.

All sorts of religious ideas can appeal to people who are spiritually hungry—but not all of these ideas lead to God. Paul warned the Colossians not to be misled by spurious teachings and practices that were being promoted in their community (Colossians 2:18,21-23). Rather, he urged them to hold "fast to the head, from whom the whole body, nourished and held together by its ligaments and sinews, grows with a growth that is from God" (2:19).

Today, many who are "spiritually open" or searching for God are attracted to anything that seems to promise heightened spiritual consciousness or contact with the supernatural. Just as in Paul's time, Christians must carefully discern what fits with Jesus and his truth and reject what is contrary to the purity of the gospel message. Aware of this need, the Catholic Church recently published a study entitled *Jesus Christ the Bearer of the Water of Life: A Christian Reflection on the "New Age."* This document points to "the need for Catholics to have an understanding of authentic Catholic doctrine and spirituality in order to properly assess New Age themes" (Foreword) and states:

> It is difficult to separate the individual elements of New Age religiosity—innocent though they may appear—from the overarching framework which permeates the whole thought-world on the *New Age* movement. The gnostic nature of this movement calls us to judge it in its entirety. From the point of view of Christian faith, it is not possible to isolate some elements of *New Age* religiosity as acceptable to Christians, while rejecting others. Since the *New Age* movement makes much of a communication with nature, of cosmic knowledge of a universal good—thereby negating the revealed contents of Christian faith—it cannot be viewed as positive or innocuous. In a cultural environment, marked by religious relativism, it is necessary to signal a warning against the attempt to place *New Age* religiosity on the same level as Christian faith, making the difference between faith and belief seem relative, thus creating greater confusion for the unwary. (4)

The study further notes,

> We find in the Letter to the Colossians and in the New Testament a doctrine of God different from that implicit in *New Age* thought: the Christian conception of God is one of

> a Trinity of Persons who has created the human race out of a desire to share the communion of Trinitarian life with creaturely persons. Properly understood, this means that authentic spirituality is not so much our search for God but God's search for us. (3.3)

Let's fix our eyes on Jesus, the source of our salvation, and pray that he protect the whole Christian people from anything that would distract us from him.

Colossians 3:1-11

1 So if you have been raised with Christ, seek the things that are
above, where Christ is, seated at the right hand of God. 2 Set your
minds on things that are above, not on things that are on earth,
3 for you have died, and your life is hidden with Christ in God.
4 When Christ who is your life is revealed, then you also will be
revealed with him in glory.
5 Put to death, therefore, whatever in you is earthly: fornication,
impurity, passion, evil desire, and greed (which is idolatry). 6 On
account of these the wrath of God is coming on those who are disobedient. 7 These are the ways you also once followed, when you
were living that life. 8 But now you must get rid of all such things—
anger, wrath, malice, slander, and abusive language from your
mouth. 9 Do not lie to one another, seeing that you have stripped
off the old self with its practices 10 and have clothed yourselves
with the new self, which is being renewed in knowledge according

to the image of its creator. [11] In that renewal there is no longer
Greek and Jew, circumcised and uncircumcised, barbarian,
Scythian, slave and free; but Christ is all and in all!

The Christians at Colossae were faced with a daunting list of vices which they were to put off: sexual impurity, greed, anger, abusive language, and lying (Colossians 3:5,8-9). Some of these things we may see in our day-to-day lives, and they can make us feel powerless. After reading these words, we may be tempted to tighten our belts, square our shoulders, and try harder to resist these sins.

In light of this tendency, we should not lose sight of the context in which these vices are to be put off, thereby reducing what we do to an exercise in self-effort: The previous passages in Colossians makes it clear that the focus of our moral activity must be Christ. Jesus—the image of the invisible God, the One in whom and for whom all was created, the One seated at God's right hand (Colossians 1:15-18; 3:1)—is the One who empowers us to turn from sin.

The Letter to the Colossians declares: "Put to death . . . whatever in you is earthly" (3:5), but in what manner? We are to put to death the earthly in us based on the truth that we "have been raised with Christ" and therefore can reject our old way of living and "seek the things that are above" (3:1). Through baptism and faith, we have died to all that is of the old order *and* have been raised up to live in the resurrection life of Christ. A profound change has been worked in us. In light of God's work, we must choose in the power of Christ to strip off the practices of the old life and live in the "new self which is being renewed in knowledge according to the image of its creator" (3:10).

The highest virtue with which we must be clothed is love, which "binds everything together" and is the truest reflection of the life of Christ within us (Colossians 3:14). As a community of faith, we should reflect an attitude of thanksgiving to God for all he has given us in Christ. Let us not lose sight of the foundational position from which we are encouraged to put off vice and put on virtue: We have been raised with Christ from the deadness of sin. Christ in us makes it possible for us to make the choices against sin and for God which distinguish us as his children.

Colossians 3:12-17

12 As God's chosen ones, holy and beloved, clothe yourselves
with compassion, kindness, humility, meekness, and patience.
13 Bear with one another and, if anyone has a complaint against
another, forgive each other; just as the Lord has forgiven you, so
you also must forgive. 14 Above all, clothe yourselves with love,
which binds everything together in perfect harmony. 15 And let the
peace of Christ rule in your hearts, to which indeed you were called
in the one body. And be thankful. 16 Let the word of Christ dwell
in you richly; teach and admonish one another in all wisdom; and
with gratitude in your hearts sing psalms, hymns, and spiritual
songs to God. 17 And whatever you do, in word or deed, do everything in the name of the Lord Jesus, giving thanks to God the
Father through him.

When the sign of the cross was traced on our foreheads and the words, "I baptize you," were spoken over us, we were immersed in Christ. Satan's hold over us was nullified, and Jesus became our source of life. Sin's iron grip on us was broken. We were made new. As God's chosen ones, living "in Christ" (Colossians 1:2), we can now live in a new way. Scripture tells us, "As many of you as were baptized into Christ have clothed yourselves with Christ" (Galatians 3:27). This is God's solemn assurance.

Our natural tendency is to think that if only we work hard enough, pray fervently enough, and persevere long enough, then someday we will be done with sin—or, at least, a few sins. But Paul entreats us to "put to death," "get rid of," "strip off" the old life (Colossians 3:5,8,9). It is a decisive act, as conclusive as severing a cord with a knife. It is an act of the will, an act of deliberate faith in God. And, because it is an act of faith, it is God's work within us that is of fundamental importance. Every time we decide to turn from sin and follow Christ, we open ourselves to the new life he gave us in baptism. Every time we face temptation, we can reaffirm our decisive, baptismal choice to put off sin and put away the old life. As we do, the Holy Spirit honors our decision by giving us the grace to persevere and see victory.

Sin is sin, and we must forsake it decisively, repeating that decision as often as necessary. Whenever we are faced with sin, we need to declare our faith. We have died with Christ, and our life is now hidden in him (Colossians 3:3). God has liberated us, and he will sustain our liberty. We can clothe ourselves with Christ (3:12,14). It is possible for us to put on his compassion, patience, and forgiveness. Jesus can rule in our hearts (3:15).

Assert your faith in God today. The more you hold to the truth that in Christ you have put off the old nature and have put on a new life, the more you will experience his consolation and peace.

"Lord Jesus, thank you for making me new. I choose to turn away from sin today. I place my trust in what you have already done for me."

Colossians 3:18–4:1

18 Wives, be subject to your husbands, as is fitting in the Lord.
19 Husbands, love your wives and never treat them harshly.
20 Children, obey your parents in everything, for this is your
acceptable duty in the Lord. 21 Fathers, do not provoke your children, or they may lose heart. 22 Slaves, obey your earthly masters in
everything, not only while being watched and in order to please
them, but wholeheartedly, fearing the Lord. 23 Whatever your task,
put yourselves into it, as done for the Lord and not for your masters, 24 since you know that from the Lord you will receive the
inheritance as your reward; you serve the Lord Christ. 25 For the
wrongdoer will be paid back for whatever wrong has been done,
and there is no partiality.
1 Masters, treat your slaves justly and fairly, for you know that
you also have a Master in heaven.

What's this about slaves obeying their masters? Why didn't Paul protest against such an immoral practice anyway? And that part about wives being subject to husbands—isn't that archaic?" So go some of our "gut" reactions when we read this passage, wondering if Paul was some kind of a reactionary or woman-hater.

Actually, Paul's ideas were quite revolutionary to his readers. The heart of his teaching was radically different from the social expectations and practices of his day. We may take offense today at the thought of submitting to another person, but in the first-century Greco-Roman world of the Colossians, the control of husbands over wives, fathers over children, and masters over slaves was complete and absolute. Obedience by subordinates was unquestioned and unquestioning. Seen in this light, Paul's exhortations were unique: Those in authority were to act with love.

Paul did not seek to undermine traditional family structures, nor did he advocate abolishing slavery. (He did, however, urge slaves to gain their freedom when possible—1 Corinthians 7:21.) He did give Christians a new perspective on how to conduct themselves within these relationships: Husbands were to love and cherish their wives. Fathers were to be gentle rather than severe with their children. Masters were to respect and treat their slaves fairly (Colossians 3:19,21; 4:1). Earlier, Paul had written that "love . . . binds everything together in perfect harmony" (3:14); now we find him giving practical advice in very concrete terms about how to express and live out that love in peace and accord.

When Paul urged the Colossians to act in love toward one another, no matter what their circumstances or position in the family, he also reminded them that by doing so, they were serving Christ, the true Lord and head of every household (Colossians 3:23). Just so for us today: When we treat other people with love, and even obey them when appropriate, it is out of our love for the Lord himself. As St. Francis de Sales pointed out, in words so similar to Paul's, "To be perfect in our vocation is nothing else than to fulfill the duties which our state of life obliges us to perform, and to accomplish them well, and only for the honor and love of God."

As you pray through this passage, ask the Holy Spirit to soften your heart and show you what love for Christ demands of you in the relationships that make up the fabric of your life: with spouse and children, with friends and neighbors, with boss and coworkers. Know that in loving all these, "you serve the Lord Christ" (3:24).

Colossians 4:2-6

2 Devote yourselves to prayer, keeping alert in it with thanksgiving. [3] At the same time pray for us as well that God will open to us
a door for the word, that we may declare the mystery of Christ, for
which I am in prison, [4] so that I may reveal it clearly, as I should.
5 Conduct yourselves wisely toward outsiders, making the most
of the time. [6] Let your speech always be gracious, seasoned with
salt, so that you may know how you ought to answer everyone.

Devote yourselves to prayer, keeping alert in it with thanksgiving.
(Colossians 4:2)

In several letters, Paul coupled prayer—especially intercessory prayer—with thanksgiving: "In everything by prayer and supplication with *thanksgiving* let your requests be made known to God" (Philippians 4:6); "I urge that supplications, prayers, intercessions and *thanksgivings* be made for everyone" (1 Timothy 2:1). God deserves our thanks simply because he *is* God, worthy of our praise and our gratitude. But Paul also knew that there are countless more reasons for us to give thanks to God when we come before him in prayer: for his love and mercy, for redeeming us from our sins, for his daily care and provision.

In a homily on this section of the Letter to the Colossians, St. John Chrysostom underscored Paul's exhortation on thanksgiving:

> This is your duty to give thanks to God in your prayers, both for the benefits you are conscious of having received and for those which God has given you without your realizing it. Thank him both for the favors you have sought from him and for those which he has done for you despite yourselves. . . . In a word, thank him for everything. (*Homilies on Colossians*, 10)

Giving thanks can transform our lives. Do you find yourself weighed down occasionally by negative thoughts and attitudes? Do you habitually focus on things you don't have, wishing for "greener grass on the other side of the fence," instead of thanking the Lord for all that he has given you? Often we take God and his gifts for granted, acting as if we have a right to them or deserve them. We may even underrate the things of God, growing too accustomed to them, and our appreciation frequently becomes jaded. But the Lord can make profound changes in us when we heed Paul's advice to couple thanksgiving with prayer.

Try it. Make a list of what you are grateful for. Then, as you pray today, read it before the Lord as a "litany" of thanksgiving to him. Try to add to your list each day. "Practice makes perfect." Regularly recounting what you're thankful for glorifies God and will transform your outlook. It breaks bad habits and forms the good habit of thanking God for his blessings. As you do, you'll be amazed to see just how many blessings you have received!

"Bless the LORD, O my soul, and all that is within me, bless his holy name. Bless the LORD, O my soul, and do not forget all his benefits!" (Psalm 103:1-2).

Colossians 4:7-18

7 Tychicus will tell you all the news about me; he is a beloved
brother, a faithful minister, and a fellow servant in the Lord. 8 I
have sent him to you for this very purpose, so that you may know
how we are and that he may encourage your hearts; 9 he is coming
with Onesimus, the faithful and beloved brother, who is one of you.
They will tell you about everything here.
10 Aristarchus my fellow prisoner greets you, as does Mark the
cousin of Barnabas, concerning whom you have received instructions—if he comes to you, welcome him. 11 And Jesus who is called
Justus greets you. These are the only ones of the circumcision
among my co-workers for the kingdom of God, and they have been
a comfort to me. 12 Epaphras, who is one of you, a servant of Christ
Jesus, greets you. He is always wrestling in his prayers on your
behalf, so that you may stand mature and fully assured in everything that God wills. 13 For I testify for him that he has worked
hard for you and for those in Laodicea and in Hierapolis. 14 Luke,
the beloved physician, and Demas greet you. 15 Give my greetings
to the brothers and sisters in Laodicea, and to Nympha and the
church in her house. 16 And when this letter has been read among
you, have it read also in the church of the Laodiceans; and see that
you read also the letter from Laodicea. 17 And say to Archippus,
"See that you complete the task that you have received in the
Lord."
18 I, Paul, write this greeting with my own hand. Remember my
chains. Grace be with you.

Tychicus, fellow servant in the Lord . . . Onesimus, beloved brother . . . Aristarchus, fellow prisoner . . . Mark, the cousin of Barnabas . . . Justus, a worker for the kingdom . . . Epaphras, a servant of Christ Jesus . . . Luke, the beloved physician . . . Demas . . . Nympha . . . Archippus. (Colossians 4:7,8,10,11,12,14,15,17)

Imagine what exciting conversion stories must belong to these men and women who had welcomed the gospel message that was setting the Mediterranean world on fire! Aristarchus was a convert Paul made in Thessalonica and had become a traveling companion of his. It's also possible that he had shared Paul's imprisonment in Ephesus (Acts 19:29; 20:4; 27:2). Nympha was, most likely, a wealthy matron—her home was large enough for her to host a Christian gathering (Colossians 4:15)—whose life had been transformed when she came to know Jesus. We can only wonder at the intriguing life histories of these first-century believers to whom we owe such a debt of gratitude as our forebears in the faith, since the New Testament tells us nothing else about them.

This roster of early Christians has come down to us because they were all friends of Paul, coworkers who shared his zeal for the gospel, men and women whom he loved dearly. Each of them had a place in his heart. Paul cared intensely about their well-being and esteemed them deeply for their labors in the Lord. Since he also knew that they loved him and were interested to hear all about his affairs, he sent Tychicus and Onesimus to the Colossians to deliver his letter and bring them personal news of him (Colossians 4:7-9).

Just as in Paul's day, the modern church is made up of men and women serving side by side for the sake of the gospel. It is the body of Christ, a living network of personal relationships. We are knit together in love. Missionaries caring for AIDS patients in West Africa, parishioners who teach RCIA classes, volunteers at the local food bank run by an interdenominational Christian board—all these people are partners with us in the gospel. They are not nameless and faceless. They are our friends, our neighbors, our relatives—and truly our brothers and sisters in the Lord.

"Thank you, Father, for all my brothers and sisters in Christ. Teach me to cherish them, just as Paul cherished his partners in the gospel."

Life in a Missionary Outpost

The First and Second Letters to the Thessalonians

An Introduction to the Letters to the Thessalonians

by Fr. Joseph A. Mindling, O.F.M. Cap.

What was it like to be the very first Christian community in an ancient pagan city? Anyone interested in getting better acquainted with the earliest converts to our faith in those challenging circumstances will find a special satisfaction in reading these two letters.

Since the correspondence of St. Paul to his churches is standardly arranged according to length—from the longest epistles to the shortest—these two writings end up somewhat inconspicuously near the end of that section of the New Testament. Nevertheless, they were composed around A.D. 50, which makes them the oldest Christian compositions to have survived from the apostolic era. They offer us a tantalizing taste of what was going on in a beleaguered missionary outpost only twenty years after Jesus had risen from the dead.

The Historical Setting. Thessalonica was a busy port town on the northwestern coast of the Aegean Sea, and in the first century one of the main highways of the Roman Empire passed through it. The volume of sea and land traffic that passed through this regional capital of Macedonia attracted a team of Christian missionaries that included Paul, Silas, and Timothy. Acts 17:1-9 preserves a brief sketch of their perilous but at least partially successful proselytizing there. They started in the influential Jewish quarter, but then—forcibly evicted from the synagogue—they preached the gospel among those who frequented the pagan shrines and temples located throughout the city.

The arrival of Christianity triggered a very polarized reaction. Some responded enthusiastically to the good news, "recognizing God's voice in the words of human messengers" (1 Thessalonians 2:13). Others wanted to stamp out this religious intrusion. Soon a politically aggressive enclave of Jewish activists staged a riot against the troop of evangelizers and the locals who were loyal to them. This forced Paul's companions to hustle him out of town for his own safety. Unfortunately, his escape left the fledgling converts to fend for themselves in very hostile surroundings.

As we learn from the letters themselves, Paul remained deeply concerned about the physical and the spiritual well-being of his minimally catechized new flock. After some frustrated attempts to revisit them, he decided to move on to the south, continuing his preaching but very preoccupied about the survival of the church back in Thessalonica. Still without word when he reached Athens, he finally risked sending Timothy back alone to check on them. Much to Paul's relief, the younger missionary returned to report that despite continued persecution, the community was still thriving. In fact, they had even become a source of inspiration for several other Christian congregations in the neighboring territories.

At this point, having continued on to Corinth, Paul penned what we call First Thessalonians. He was eager to renew and strengthen his special relationship with the Thessalonians, to assure them of his loving concern, and to respond to some questions they had sent back to him with his trusted envoy. We have no certain knowledge about how much time elapsed between the sending of the first letter and the second. Tradition tells us that the interval was not long—perhaps only a matter of a few months or even weeks. Even in that short period, however, further developments were reported back to the apostle.

These prompted him to reiterate some of the still smoldering issues he had addressed in his first letter, but also to raise some new points in the letter now known as Second Thessalonians.

As far as we can tell, Paul never thought of his pastoral letters being read and pondered by the people of God long after his death, and the New Testament probably contains only a small sampling of all that he wrote. Nevertheless, although the circumstances that prompted these compositions were real and very time-conditioned, the Holy Spirit moved this eloquent pastor to preserve his thoughts in a way that has proved to be instructive and inspiring for countless believers ever since. Let's examine a few of the prominent teachings in the letters to the Thessalonians that have made them sources of wisdom and encouragement down through the ages.

Paul's Self-Image as a Member of the Thessalonian Family. Paul writes to his converts both as the one who had first proclaimed the faith to them, and as God's legate, still responsible for helping them to solidify their faith and to grow in grace and virtue. He compares himself to a "father with his children" (1 Thessalonians 2:11), to "a nursing mother with her little ones" (2:7), and even to an "orphan" (2:17) when he is separated from them. Readers today, accustomed to pastoral letters that are addressed in more general terms to perhaps thousands of anonymous believers in a diocese, may find themselves surprised by Paul's spiritual intimacy and his references to shared personal experiences with recently baptized Christians.

He refers unabashedly to his own ongoing role as an authority figure for them, and he also instructs them to respect those who work among them, exercising the office of religious leadership within the church. But he comes across even more emphatically as a friend, compassionately concerned about the hardships and challenges they are experiencing. Paul is enthusiastic about the spiritual growth Timothy has seen, evidence testifying to what had to be the effective presence of the Holy Spirit guiding their deliberations and activities. He is not silent about their shortcomings, but his confidence in them still moves him to challenge the community to continued progress and new growth.

Paul's comments about the efforts of this new group of believers to purify their still limited understanding of the faith and to persevere in their commitment are a strong reminder of the value of our own personal "history of belief"—as individuals and as communities. Like the majority of Christians today who take their baptism seriously, the Thessalonians were working to solidify their union with Christ, even though they were surrounded by many who had not "turned from idols to serve the living and true God" (1 Thessalonians 1:9). Some of their fellow citizens mocked and mistreated them for involving themselves with this foreign religion that had triggered such hostility in the local Hebrew congregation. Acts 17:5-9 offers a description of one individual and his household who were physically attacked in the public forum for daring to offer hospitality and acceptance to Christian missionaries.

The Inevitability of the Cross. Paul comes back to this theme of trial and tribulation in several passages, and he himself was no stranger to persecution. Even when he first appeared in Thessalonica, he had been fleeing "shameful treatment in Philippi" (1 Thessalonians 2:2) and he recalls how, from the very beginning, the Thessalonians had "received the word in great affliction." In persevering despite such abuse, these Gentile converts in distant Macedonia were not only sharing in Paul's hardship; he praises them for following in the footsteps of their sister churches who were enduring similar suffering in the Holy Land.

Instead of being surprised or unduly disheartened at this, Paul reminds them how he had predicted that this aspect of the cross would be an unavoidable consequence of embracing the gospel:

> Indeed, you yourselves know that this is what we are destined for. In fact, when we were with you we told you beforehand that we were to suffer persecution; and so it turned out, as you know. (1 Thessalonians 3:3-5)

Able to speak credibly because of his own personal experience, Paul urges them "not to repay evil for evil" (1 Thessalonians 5:15)—even though that might be a natural temptation. Rather, they are to "encourage one another and build one another up" (5:11), as they have been doing. After all, the reason he had sent Timothy back to them was "to strengthen and encourage them for the sake of their faith, so that no one would be shaken by these persecutions" (3:2-3). He is very realistic in acknowledging what the Thessalonians are going through, including their personal struggles to comply with Christian sexual norms. Yet, through it all, he models for them an attitude of determined perseverance, inspired by his unwavering trust in Jesus' death and resurrection.

Concerns about the Second Coming and the Afterlife. Perhaps because Paul had not been able to complete their initial instructions, some of his new converts had distorted the apostle's exhortation to be ready "at any time" for Jesus' final coming, turning it into a conviction that the end of the world was going to take place in the very near future. Moreover, as death overtook a number of their fellow believers, some were worrying that those who were not alive at Christ's glorious return would be deprived of the blessed afterlife they had hoped for. Still others were spreading false rumors that Paul had sent another letter, teaching that somehow the Second Coming had already taken place.

Both of his authentic epistles respond to these concerns by reviewing the basics of what Paul had already taught and then by correcting the misconceptions that had surfaced. Using imagery from some of the dramatic word pictures in the Old Testament, he describes Jesus' future coming as a descent from the heavens, accompanied with trumpet blasts, a powerful angelic retinue, and a backdrop of fire. Educated Christians have commonly understood such apocalyptic language as figurative rather than literal. Nevertheless, these striking images have served as a very effective means down through the centuries to communicate, to both the simple and the sophisticated, the awesome nature of the coming Day of the Lord.

Paul tried to calm the inappropriate anxieties of the Thessalonians by reassuring them that all human beings will be awakened and participate in the final resurrection. He insists, however, that the exact day and hour of the climax of human history have not been revealed, and that the End Time will be preceded by a major conflict between the forces of good and evil. This cosmic battle—hardly an event that could have already happened without the nervous Thessalonians noticing it—is being held in check by the Lord of History through agents beyond our ken. Thus, like all births and deaths, the conclusion of the present era and the beginning of the future age will certainly come, but the exact timing remains as unpredictable as "a thief in the night" (1 Thessalonians 5:2). In the meantime, the only way to be prepared is to conform ourselves to Christ.

Christians, Pull Your Own Weight, Spiritually and Materially. Paul is well known as the outspoken opponent of any claim that salvation could be "earned" simply by performing certain religious "works." On the other hand, his admonitions to the Thessalonians show that he could be just as adamant about the need to engage in honest labor and to cooperate with God's Spirit in the pursuit of holiness. When some in the Macedonian church decided that they would just let others in the community feed and support them while they waited around for Jesus to come again, Paul's reaction was blunt: "Anyone living in idleness should do their work quietly and earn their own living" (2 Thessalo-nians 3:12). "Anyone unwilling to work should not eat!" (3:10).

The apostle could say this in good conscience, since while preaching at Thessalonica he had always earned his keep by working with his own hands. True to his regular custom, he had refused to accept any financial compensation from them, even though he had every right to such support as a herald of the good news who evangelized day and night. Thus, he could urge them without embarrassment to imitate his own diligence and to avoid ever becoming an unjust drain on the community's resources—especially while trying to justify such shameful cadging on the basis of faulty theology.

Know That You Are Loved. Before approaching the reflections in the individual sections of this devotional commentary, you might do well just to read through these epistles in your own Bible. They are short enough that you can easily finish each of them in one sitting, as they were surely read when they first arrived. As you do so, notice how many ways Paul finds to voice his warm concern and fondness for the Thessalonians in Christ. This is his most moving message. In our time, when explicit statements of caring and affection are often few and far between, you will also be pleased to see how disarmingly the apostle captures this Christian love in words that can still touch hearts today.

1 Thessalonians 1:1-10

1 Paul, Silvanus, and Timothy,
To the church of the Thessalonians in God the Father and the
Lord Jesus Christ:
Grace to you and peace.
2 We always give thanks to God for all of you and mention you
in our prayers, constantly 3 remembering before our God and
Father your work of faith and labor of love and steadfastness of
hope in our Lord Jesus Christ. 4 For we know, brothers and sisters
beloved by God, that he has chosen you, 5 because our message of
the gospel came to you not in word only, but also in power and in
the Holy Spirit and with full conviction; just as you know what
kind of persons we proved to be among you for your sake. 6 And
you became imitators of us and of the Lord, for in spite of persecution you received the word with joy inspired by the Holy Spirit, 7 so
that you became an example to all the believers in Macedonia and
in Achaia. 8 For the word of the Lord has sounded forth from you
not only in Macedonia and Achaia, but in every place your faith in
God has become known, so that we have no need to speak about it.
9 For the people of those regions report about us what kind of welcome we had among you, and how you turned to God from idols, to
serve a living and true God, 10 and to wait for his Son from heaven,
whom he raised from the dead—Jesus, who rescues us from the
wrath that is coming.

Located in the province of Macedonia in the northern Greek peninsula, Thessalonica was a center of Roman administration and a prosperous port city. Paul and his companions established the church there on their second missionary journey (Acts 17:1-9). The letter that Paul, Silvanus, and Timothy wrote to this church around A.D. 50 is probably the oldest existing Christian document, and it gives us a fascinating glimpse of Christianity's earliest years.

The gospel message came to the Thessalonians "not in word only, but also in power and in the Holy Spirit and with full conviction" (1 Thessalonians 1:5). The Thessalonians were chosen by God because the Holy Spirit opened up their hearts to listen, believe, and accept God's truth as it was preached by the apostles. The Spirit convicted them of their idolatry and filled them with a desire to live for Christ, whose return they eagerly anticipated (1:9-10).

Because the Thessalonians wholeheartedly accepted the gospel, their lives exhibited the three most important Christian virtues: faith, hope, and love (1 Thessalonians 1:3). The Holy Spirit empowered them to imitate Jesus by joyfully persevering in their faith despite persecution. Not only did they maintain their faith, but their love for God and each other made them a powerful witness to their neighbors, and of the transforming power of the gospel.

God's power is available in our lives as well if we open our hearts to the Spirit's revelation of Jesus. On our own, we are powerless against the sinful desires of the flesh, but by God's power given to us through the cross of Christ, we can be freed from sin and conformed to the image of Jesus, our Savior. As we turn to God each day, the powers of Satan, sin, and death are crushed under the might of God's powers. Like the Thessalonians, we too are enabled to believe and obey Jesus' command to love God and one another. Through our example, the Holy Spirit will allow the gospel to come with power upon all we meet, enabling them to repent of sin and receive God's love, forgiveness, and eternal life.

"Lord, let your power transform our lives and embolden us to preach your gospel so that all may be saved."

1 Thessalonians 2:1-8

1 You yourselves know, brothers and sisters, that our coming to
you was not in vain, 2 but though we had already suffered and been
shamefully mistreated at Philippi, as you know, we had courage in
our God to declare to you the gospel of God in spite of great opposition. 3 For our appeal does not spring from deceit or impure
motives or trickery, 4 but just as we have been approved by God to
be entrusted with the message of the gospel, even so we speak, not
to please mortals, but to please God who tests our hearts. 5 As you
know and as God is our witness, we never came with words of flat-
tery or with a pretext for greed; 6 nor did we seek praise from mortals, whether from you or from others, 7 though we might have
made demands as apostles of Christ. But we were gentle among
you, like a nurse tenderly caring for her own children. 8 So deeply
do we care for you that we are determined to share with you not
only the gospel of God but also our own selves, because you have
become very dear to us.

St. Paul exhorted men and women to please God rather than mortals (1 Thessalonians 2:4), but our actions are often the opposite. Our concern is more often about how we appear to others than in pleasing God. We often live as though we are ashamed of the gospel; we fail to proclaim it when opportunities present themselves because we do not want to be considered religious fanatics or naïve and unsophisticated. How easy it is to lay the responsibility of evangelization on the clergy or others in religious life.

We don't have to be theologians or Scripture scholars in order to proclaim the goods news effectively. St. Paul said to the Corinthians: "I decided to know nothing among you except Jesus Christ, and him crucified. . . . My speech and my proclamation were not with plausible words of wisdom, but with a demonstration of the Spirit and of power" (1 Corinthians 2:2,4).

All of those who have accepted the gospel are called by God to proclaim it to others, especially to family, friends, and people for whom they have some responsibility. Unbelievers may be lost forever for lack of someone to share the gospel with them. What is more important: to be quiet for fear of offending them and embarrassing ourselves, or to speak out in love and concern for their salvation? Will we please humans or please God?

St. Paul described how to share the gospel. He said we need to speak the truth with love and with the gentleness of a nursing mother (1 Thessalonians 2:7-8). If you feel unprepared and unqualified to do this, remember that the Holy Spirit will give you the words that those you are speaking with need to hear (Matthew 10:19-20). God has commissioned us to announce the good news of his Son, Jesus Christ. Even the most hardened heart can be changed by the truth of the gospel proclaimed in love. Let us not be prevented by fear or pride from spreading the word of salvation in Christ Jesus.

"Spirit of the living God, come and give me wisdom and courage. Lead me as I share the truth of Jesus with others. Give me the words to say and the love to say them."

1 Thessalonians 2:9-13

9 You remember our labor and toil, brothers and sisters; we
worked night and day, so that we might not burden any of you
while we proclaimed to you the gospel of God. 10 You are witnesses,
and God also, how pure, upright, and blameless our conduct was
toward you believers. 11 As you know, we dealt with each one of
you like a father with his children, 12 urging and encouraging you
and pleading that you lead a life worthy of God, who calls you into
his own kingdom and glory.
13 We also constantly give thanks to God for this, that when you
received the word of God that you heard from us, you accepted it
not as a human word but as what it really is, God's word, which is
also at work in you believers.

Paul supported himself by making tents and other leather goods. It is also likely that much of his ministry was done in the course of his workday. This was the traditional rabbinic practice of the times, and a necessity for Paul for several reasons: The Jerusalem church was too poor to finance his efforts, his Jewish friends and relatives would certainly not abet him in his work of preaching Christ, and he was traveling to places where there were (as yet) no converts to rely on for support.

As he labored for the upbuilding of the church, Paul's work bore the mark of God. It was "pure, upright, and blameless" (1 Thessalonians 2:10), reflecting not the work of the flesh, but that of the spirit. As such, it stands as a model for us.

In our own time, the work of building up the church still entails labor and toil out of the spirit rather than the flesh. There are among the faithful intelligent minds which can help to interpret critical issues of the day; musicians and others with artistic talent to assist at our liturgical services; gifted organizers who can rally people and exhort them to do their best; people who can fix things; people who can bake, and so on. Because Christ came to redeem *all* things, the work of the church encompasses *all* things, but always must be accomplished through the Spirit.

In a similar way, we are called to labor and toil as we undertake the responsibility of working for the salvation of our families (what the Second Vatican Council termed the "domestic church"). A good way to start is to spend time praying for family members. Husbands and wives can confer on priorities: To what should they devote their time? What plans can be made for the children? Consider how a teacher spends hours preparing lessons in order to be able to explain the subject most effectively to the students. The work of the domestic church is no less demanding, but God prepares spouses for it in the Sacrament of Marriage.

"Father, bless the work of the church and make her a beautiful bride for your Son. Let us participate in this work in our parishes and in our families. May our efforts be a work of the Spirit and bear fruit for Jesus."

1 Thessalonians 2:14-16

14 For you, brothers and sisters, became imitators of the churches
of God in Christ Jesus that are in Judea, for you suffered the same
things from your own compatriots as they did from the Jews, 15 who
killed both the Lord Jesus and the prophets, and drove us out; they
displease God and oppose everyone 16 by hindering us from speaking to the Gentiles so that they may be saved. Thus they have constantly been filling up the measure of their sins; but God's wrath
has overtaken them at last.

He makes us look bad!" "I wish she wasn't such a goody-two-shoes. She might fit in better!" It's a universal rule: No matter how hard we try, we can't make everyone happy. Especially when we're trying to live the Christian life, we will offend some people, and St. Paul assures us that we will be persecuted.

Some scholars believe that because they seem to interrupt the thought flow of this chapter, these few verses may have been inserted into Paul's letter at a later time. If that's the case, then the writer of this section was encouraging new Christians a few decades after Paul's death, telling them that they too followed in the steps of the first generation of believers who endured persecution! While this section reflects a first-century outlook, the same point is just as true for us today: There will always be those who take offense at the gospel and want it silenced.

St. Gregory the Great once said: "Being despised by evildoers is a mark of approval, because when we begin to displease those who displease God, it is a sign that we are to some degree righteous"

(*Homilies on Ezekiel*, 9,12). Only God knows people's hearts; but when we are punished or ostracized for doing what is right, we know we are on the right track. We may not want this type of "approval," but as Christians we should not be surprised by it. Jesus himself told us: "If the world hates you, be aware that it hated me before it hated you" (John 15:18).

While the early believers endured physical persecution and threats of death, very few of us will experience such things. The persecution we experience is more likely to be subtle: A father may worry about the ramifications of speaking out at work, or a family finds their new neighbor avoiding them because they are open about their faith. Perhaps a student is not part of the "in crowd" because he or she is not promiscuous, or coworkers reject an associate who does not join in complaining about the boss.

Of course, there are many believers in the world today who do face severe persecution for their faith. No matter what form, persecution comes from the same source: the evil one who hates the truth. But as we hold fast to Jesus, we can know that he will stand beside us in persecution.

"Lord Jesus, I ask for your strength to stand firm in the gospel even when it requires suffering. Walk beside me, and even more, walk beside those who today will face life-and-death choices in their faith. May we all rejoice before you in your kingdom!"

1 Thessalonians 2:17-20

17 As for us, brothers and sisters, when, for a short time, we were
made orphans by being separated from you—in person, not in

heart—we longed with great eagerness to see you face to face. [18] For
we wanted to come to you—certainly I, Paul, wanted to again and
again—but Satan blocked our way. [19] For what is our hope or joy or
crown of boasting before our Lord Jesus at his coming? Is it not you?
[20] Yes, you are our glory and joy!

You are our glory and joy! (1 Thessalonians 2:20)

Imagine proud parents, watching with joy as their son performs at a piano recital, or their daughter brings home a paper marked with an "A." The same feeling flows when young athletes give their all in a hard-fought soccer match, or even when a youngster makes the surprising decision to share a favorite toy. Any parent's heart swells with pride.

On a grander scale, St. Paul likens his feelings for the Thessalonians to a city governor waiting for the return of the king and his entourage, ready to itemize the achievements of the city under his stewardship. Paul looks toward the coming of Jesus, the Parousia—a Greek term which in ancient times referred to the formal entry of a ruler into a city—with great pride in the Thessalonians. He waits to see them shine before the Lord, and bask in it as their spiritual father.

Despite the fact that he preached to thousands and helped to found many churches, Paul had very personal feelings for each of them. He wanted to see them grow in holiness, following the example he lived out, and rejoice in their heavenly reward. They are, after all, his "joy" and "crown" (1 Thessalonians 2:19; Philippians 4:1)!

What about us? Do we ever think of the pastors who have been involved in our lives, giving of themselves, and praying for our spiritual growth? Perhaps we should invite them to dinner in thanks for their role in our lives, or find some other way to express our gratitude and solidarity with them. And how do we feel toward others in our parishes? We may not have a position of leadership or authority, but in the spirit of brotherhood, we all can pray fervently and long for their growth in holiness as eagerly as Paul did for the Thessalonians.

When Jesus comes again, we will account for our actions toward others, even things neglected through indifference. What a wonderful influence we can be on the church now—and what hope we can have when Jesus returns—if we take the time to pray for the church. As the church grows in holiness, we ourselves will have a "crown of boasting," knowing that we have played an integral part!

"Lord, I thank you for those pastors who have so powerfully influenced my life! Help me to be a good example to others, and inspire me to be eager in my prayer for the church."

1 Thessalonians 3:1-6

1 Therefore when we could bear it no longer, we decided to be
left alone in Athens; 2 and we sent Timothy, our brother and co-
worker for God in proclaiming the gospel of Christ, to strengthen
and encourage you for the sake of your faith, 3 so that no one would
be shaken by these persecutions. Indeed, you yourselves know that
this is what we are destined for. 4 In fact, when we were with you,
we told you beforehand that we were to suffer persecution; so it
turned out, as you know. 5 For this reason, when I could bear it no
longer, I sent to find out about your faith; I was afraid that somehow the tempter had tempted you and that our labor had been in
vain.

6 But Timothy has just now come to us from you, and has brought us the good news of your faith and love. He has told us also that you always remember us kindly and long to see us—just as we long to see you.

A man sits by the telephone, nervously drumming his fingers on the table. He rises and begins to pace the floor, looking at the clock. He peers out the window. Evidently, he is waiting for news from someone important. When he can stand it no longer, he sends his son out with the car keys in the quest for a report.

St. Paul was so worried that the Thessalonians would lose faith in the heat of persecution that he sent Timothy to strengthen and encourage their faith and determination to hold fast to the Lord. Losing Timothy meant that Paul would be without the support of his "co-worker . . . in proclaiming the gospel" (1 Thessalonians 3:2). But his concern for this young group of believers outweighed personal interest, and he willingly sent Timothy with the hope that the words of his trusted protégé would shore them up.

Paul's willingness to be left alone for the sake of someone else's welfare may give us pause. How concerned are we when we hear about someone suffering for his or her faith? It's one thing to offer prayers for that person, but it's another to talk to them, offering them the human contact that is so important when someone is suffering. Who knows? One brief word of support may make all the difference in that person's faith life.

All around the world, people are suffering physical violence, imprisonment, and even death because they are Christians. We'll never be able to offer this kind of personal support to all of them! But there are plenty of opportunities in our own neighborhoods and parishes to imitate Timothy's ministry of encouragement and exhortation. Even those who are not suffering external persecution but are facing a particularly strong battle against sin—these too need our presence. These too need someone to show them that Jesus is with them.

Not all of us will have Paul's intense concern for the whole church. However, any time we try to encourage others in their faith or pray for those being persecuted, we ourselves are comforted and strengthened in our own faith. What's more, the witness of someone else standing firm in the faith can be a powerful source of encouragement when we face our own times of trial and suffering for Jesus. When we lend our support to others, we can be sure that God will provide for us in our own time of need.

"Thank you, Holy Spirit, that you uphold the church! We praise you because you are close to those being persecuted. You give us the privilege in comforting others just as you comfort them in their suffering."

1 Thessalonians 3:7-13

[7] For this reason, brothers and sisters, during all our distress and
persecution we have been encouraged about you through your
faith. [8] For we now live, if you continue to stand firm in the Lord.
[9] How can we thank God enough for you in return for all the joy
that we feel before our God because of you? [10] Night and day we
pray most earnestly that we may see you face to face and restore
whatever is lacking in your faith.
[11] Now may our God and Father himself and our Lord Jesus direct
our way to you. [12] And may the Lord make you increase and

abound in love for one another and for all, just as we abound in love for you. [13] And may he so strengthen your hearts in holiness that you may be blameless before our God and Father at the coming of our Lord Jesus with all his saints.

Paul's prayer here reflects more than just a fatherly affection for a church he had established (Acts 17:1-10). He eagerly desired to see his brothers and sisters in Thessalonica because he was so grateful to God for their faith; he wanted to encourage them in their Christian lives. Paul's prayer reveals his primary concerns for them—concerns which reflect a heavenly vision of God and a deep longing that this vision would become a reality in their lives.

He first prayed that the Lord would direct his way to them so that he could "restore whatever is lacking" in their faith (1 Thessalonians 3:10-11). Above everything, Paul wanted them to be filled with the Spirit, free from bondage to sin, so that they could know God's life. To say that something was lacking in their faith does not mean that they had lost whatever faith they once had. It could mean that there was *more* they could learn, *more* grace they could receive, *deeper* deliverance and *more* power over sin. Like the Father who loved them, Paul could not rest until they had received *everything* God wanted to give them.

Secondly, Paul prayed that the Lord would *increase* their love for each other and for everyone (1 Thessalonians 3:12). Faith is nothing if it doesn't manifest itself in an *ever-deepening* love, a *growing* reflection of God's love for his children (Galatians 5:6). Everything else—important though it may have been—was secondary to the questions of whether they were motivated by God's love and could manifest this love to others.

Finally, Paul prayed that they would be fully prepared for Jesus' return in glory (1 Thessalonians 3:13). Here again, Paul's words reflect his heavenly vision. We are not made for this world only, but for heaven, for godly life. We can grow closer to Christ and experience his life growing in us every day. Through prayer, the word of God, and fellowship, we can allow the Spirit to form Christ in us, making us like the eternal Son, who himself is the image of the invisible God. This is the holiness Paul prayed for.

Try to spend some time today examining your heart and asking the Spirit to give you a heavenly vision. In humility, open your heart and ask God to strengthen your faith and increase your love so that you can stand in hope of his Second Coming, eagerly desiring union with him.

1 Thessalonians 4:1-8

[1] Finally, brothers and sisters, we ask and urge you in the Lord
Jesus that, as you learned from us how you ought to live and to please
God (as, in fact, you are doing), you should do so more and more.
[2] For you know what instructions we gave you through the Lord
Jesus. [3] For this is the will of God, your sanctification: that you
abstain from fornication; [4] that each one of you know how to control
your own body in holiness and honor, [5] not with lustful passion, like
the Gentiles who do not know God; [6] that no one wrong or exploit a
brother or sister in this matter, because the Lord is an avenger in all
these things, just as we have already told you beforehand and
solemnly warned you. [7] For God did not call us to impurity but in
holiness. [8] Therefore whoever rejects this rejects not human authority but God, who also gives his Holy Spirit to you.

Moved by his affection for them, Paul urged the Thessalonians to hold fast to all that he had told them, not only about faith in Jesus Christ but also about how to live in a way pleasing to God (1 Thessalonians 4:1). However, since he had been forced to leave Thessalonica hastily while still in the early stages of establishing the community there (Acts 17:1-13), Paul knew that the new believers—most of whom came from a pagan background—lacked much basic teaching.

Though strong in their faith and love (1 Thessalonians 3:6), some of these new converts had not fully understood that the message of salvation carried with it practical implications for everyday life, including matters such as sexual conduct. So Paul reminded them of God's design for human sexuality and exhorted them to avoid immoral behavior. God is holy, and he wants his people to be holy, too!

This wasn't always easy. The believers in Thessalonica lived in the most cosmopolitan city in Macedonia. Every day they faced temptations against the purity and holiness God called them to (1 Thessalonians 4:3-7). Today we find ourselves in a similar situation. Sex outside of marriage is widely accepted. Pornography and adultery have become commonplace. Abortion as a means of contraception is gaining acceptance. In such an environment, we are surrounded by temptations and may find it difficult to restrain inclinations toward lustful thoughts, provocative speech, and impure behavior.

All is not lost. Almighty God has given us his Spirit to empower us against sin and safeguard our purity. And through this Spirit, our Father offers us his mercy and healing if we should fall. As we grow in our faith and love for God, we become increasingly sensitive to the movements of his Spirit within us. We learn to recognize more quickly when we have offended him, and we are more eager to confess our sins and be set free. Let's remain close to the Lord so that his will for us, our sanctification, will be fully accomplished (1 Thessalonians 4:3-6).

"Holy Spirit, purify my heart and mind so I can live a life pleasing to God in every way. Help me to turn away from sin and strengthen all that is good in me. Give me grace to live in your purity now, so that I may live forever with you."

1 Thessalonians 4:9-12

9 Now concerning love of the brothers and sisters, you do not
need to have anyone write to you, for you yourselves have been
taught by God to love one another; 10 and indeed you do love all
the brothers and sisters throughout Macedonia. But we urge you,
beloved, to do so more and more, 11 to aspire to live quietly, to
mind your own affairs, and to work with your hands, as we directed
you, 12 so that you may behave properly toward outsiders and be
dependent on no one.

God did not intend that we be alone, and he gives us many opportunities to develop relationships—with family, friends, neighbors, and coworkers. The question we should ask is whether our relationships help or hinder our Christian life. God created us in love for love. His nature is love, and we are called into fellowship with him and with his children. In baptism, we are incorporated into the family of God. Jesus said that the distinctive mark of his disciples would be their love for one another.

St. Thomas Aquinas defined charity as "friendship with God," and he described the work of the Holy Spirit as a work of friendship (*Summa Contra Gentiles*, 1.21-22). The apostle Paul addressed all Christians as "brethren," which means "brothers and sisters who belong to the same family." That is why Paul exhorted us to love one another more and more. We are members of one family, and our love for one another is not only a pleasant thing; it actually builds the kingdom of God!

The saints give us numerous examples of Christian love. For instance, Thomas More was an eminent statesman in sixteenth-century England, but he loved pauper and king equally. His enemies could find no fault in him because he treated all with the utmost kindness. Blessed Teresa of Calcutta is another example. Everyone found love, acceptance, and friendship with this humble servant of God. Her selfless love and compassion for the poor and downtrodden continue to challenge us to examine how we love others.

It is a great benefit to have close relationships with one or more "brothers or sisters in the Lord" with whom we can pray and share about God's work in our lives. We can even help remind each other about the things God puts on our hearts to do for him. Let us seek out friends who want to grow in faith, hope, and love and be strengthened in times of difficulty. Let us ask the Lord to show us how to love everyone, and give us close, personal friends who can strengthen our faith.

"Heavenly Father, you created us in love for love. Break down the walls of hostility and division that separate us. Unite us in Jesus so that we may be a sign of the unity you want for all of us."

1 Thessalonians 4:13-18

13 But we do not want you to be uninformed, brothers and sisters,
about those who have died, so that you may not grieve as others do
who have no hope. 14 For since we believe that Jesus died and rose
again, even so, through Jesus, God will bring with him those who
have died. 15 For this we declare to you by the word of the Lord,
that we who are alive, who are left until the coming of the Lord,
will by no means precede those who have died. 16 For the Lord himself, with a cry of command, with the archangel's call and with the
sound of God's trumpet, will descend from heaven, and the dead in
Christ will rise first. 17 Then we who are alive, who are left, will be
caught up in the clouds together with them to meet the Lord in the
air; and so we will be with the Lord forever. 18 Therefore encourage
one another with these words.

The reality of the Second Coming of Christ should be a source of hope and encouragement to all Christians. The Thessalonians were feeling some confusion about the destiny of their loved ones who had died. They also wondered what would happen to those who would be alive when Jesus came again. Jesus had promised to return (John 14:3), and so Paul was confident that all would experience the glory of the resurrected life: "For as all die in Adam, so all will be made alive in Christ" (1 Corinthians 15:22).

The word *parousia* (from the Greek for "presence" or "arrival") is sometimes used to describe Jesus' Second Coming. The Parousia is the time of the resurrection of the dead when the righteous will be joined with Christ (1 Corinthians 15:21-23). To the Thessalonians, Paul wrote:

"For the Lord himself, with a cry of command, with the archangel's call and with the sound of God's trumpet, will descend from heaven, and the dead in Christ will rise first" (1 Thessalonians 4:16).

Paul taught that Christians should await the Second Coming with hope and expectancy. However, the truth of Jesus' return sometimes becomes a distant reality that hardly affects our everyday lives. We also don't see the importance of Jesus coming to take us, body and soul, into heaven. How can the Second Coming be awaited with the eager anticipation Paul exhorted us to have?

In the Lord's Prayer, we pray for the coming of the Lord's kingdom—"Thy kingdom come, thy will be done." This prayer can help focus our thoughts on Jesus' Second Coming. Elsewhere we are taught how we are to live while awaiting this event: "For the grace of God has appeared, bringing salvation to all, training us to renounce impiety and worldly passions, and in the present age to live lives that are self-controlled, upright, and godly, while we wait for the blessed hope and the manifestation of the glory of our great God and Savior, Jesus Christ" (Titus 2:11-13).

St. Augustine encouraged the faithful to allow the hope of the Second Coming to be a source of joy for them:

> Then there will be great and complete joy, for it will be joy that feeds not on hope but on the reality. Yet even now, before the reality is given to us, let us rejoice in the Lord, because hope that will later be fulfilled already brings no little joy. (*Sermon* 21)

May we rejoice in the reality of what is to come.

1 Thessalonians 5:1-11

1 Now concerning the times and the seasons, brothers and sisters, you do not need to have anything written to you. 2 For you
yourselves know very well that the day of the Lord will come like
a thief in the night. 3 When they say, "There is peace and security," then sudden destruction will come upon them, as labor
pains come upon a pregnant woman, and there will be no escape!
4 But you, beloved, are not in darkness, for that day to surprise
you like a thief; 5 for you are all children of light and children of
the day; we are not of the night or of darkness. 6 So then let us
not fall asleep as others do, but let us keep awake and be sober;
7 for those who sleep sleep at night, and those who are drunk get
drunk at night. 8 But since we belong to the day, let us be sober,
and put on the breastplate of faith and love, and for a helmet the
hope of salvation. 9 For God has destined us not for wrath but for
obtaining salvation through our Lord Jesus Christ, 10 who died for
us, so that whether we are awake or asleep we may live with him.
11 Therefore encourage one another and build up each other, as
indeed you are doing.

St. Paul taught that the Day of the Lord will come as suddenly and surely as labor pains come to a woman with child. Those in spiritual darkness will be surprised and unprepared. They will be expecting security and peace when, like a thief in the night, the end will come. This situation will pose a great threat to those living in darkness, and we pray that they turn to the Lord, who is all merciful, even in those last moments.

But this is not what God has destined for those who are in Christ. They know that their salvation is won and held secure by the blood of Jesus. By God's grace they are growing spiritually, coming more into the light, and separating themselves from the darkness of sin. "Children of light" (1 Thessalonians 5:5), they remain alert and prepared. They encourage one another and live in the faith and hope of Jesus coming again.

God asks us to prepare ourselves for the One who loves us and whom we love. Imagine what it would be like if your husband or wife were about to return home from a long trip. You might put on some good clothes and try to make your home look especially presentable. You might even have a special gift waiting. You would be alert and prepared—not out of fear, but because someone you love is coming back to you. How much more prepared should we be for the Lord, who died so that we could be filled with divine love? How much more for the One who has captured our hearts and will take us to eternal happiness and joy?

Let us pray today that all those living in darkness are brought into Jesus' light. Let's join our hearts with the psalmist as we pray and prepare for the Second Coming of Christ: "The LORD is my light and my salvation; whom shall I fear? The LORD is the stronghold of my life; of whom shall I be afraid? . . . One thing I asked of the LORD, . . . to live in the house of the LORD all the days of my life, to behold the beauty of the LORD" (Psalm 27:1,4).

"Lord, bring those in spiritual darkness into your light."

1 Thessalonians 5:12-22

12 But we appeal to you, brothers and sisters, to respect those who
labor among you, and have charge of you in the Lord and admonish
you; 13 esteem them very highly in love because of their work. Be at
peace among yourselves. 14 And we urge you, beloved, to admonish
the idlers, encourage the fainthearted, help the weak, be patient with
all of them. 15 See that none of you repays evil for evil, but always
seek to do good to one another and to all. 16 Rejoice always, 17 pray
without ceasing, 18 give thanks in all circumstances; for this is the
will of God in Christ Jesus for you. 19 Do not quench the Spirit.
20 Do not despise the words of prophets, 21 but test everything; hold
fast to what is good; 22 abstain from every form of evil.

Respect those who . . . have charge of you in the Lord.
(1 Thessalonians 5:12)

These words can ring hollow: Esteem those in authority? We see their human weaknesses and failures. We may have problems with their policies, or with their ability to carry out what they said they would do. We may even have been hurt personally by someone in authority and feel angry. Not only that, we are bombarded with cultural messages to challenge authority and distrust it. How can we be expected to respect those in authority?

When Paul talked about respect, he did not mean that we should ignore the problems we see—see especially verse 14. But we are called upon to "be patient" even in the midst of trying to work things out. Paul tells us not to repay evil for evil; always seek to do good to all; give thanks no matter what; and pray without ceasing. Again, we may shake our heads and think it is impossible in "the real world"—nothing more than platitudes for the naïve.

What a mistake it would be to stop here! God knows our circumstances and even our cynicism. But he holds out to us an amazing opportunity. We can actually bring good into circumstances touched by irresponsibility, ill will, and even evil itself. How? By living in the Holy Spirit! It is God's will for us to hold fast to what is good and abstain from evil, because that is how we can bring the light of Christ into each and every situation and transform it. As the Holy Spirit moves in us, we will be raised above our concerns, complaints, and problems and see them from a heavenly perspective. We will gain a heart of wisdom to know how to love and forgive, even as we make our own contribution to change that which needs changing.

This perspective does not ignore the problems we may have experienced or the weaknesses that we see. What it does is help us to see as God does. He longs for his followers to be light to the world, salt to the earth—and it can happen as we allow the Holy Spirit to work through us. We can pray for the wayward pastor, encourage the dejected parishioner, help the wounded. God knows the good we can do. And he promises that as we follow him, his vision for the church will become a reality.

"Lord, seated above the heavens, we praise you in your majesty! You are raised above all earthly thrones and dominions. You have all power. Yet you choose to allow us—sinful men and women—to participate in your plans for good in this world. What a privilege! Raise our thoughts up to the heavens with you so that we can all become your instruments of transformation."

1 Thessalonians 5:23-28

23 May the God of peace himself sanctify you entirely; and may
your spirit and soul and body be kept sound and blameless at the
coming of our Lord Jesus Christ. 24 The one who calls you is faithful, and he will do this.
25 Beloved, pray for us.
26 Greet all the brothers and sisters with a holy kiss. 27 I solemnly
command you by the Lord that this letter be read to all of them.
28 The grace of our Lord Jesus Christ be with you.

The one who calls you is faithful, and he will do this. (1 Thessalonians 5:24)

Heavenly Father, I know that you call me to be holy. I know that this is your permanent attitude and not just a one-time calling. Yet so often, I feel completely inadequate to respond. You want to see me wholly sanctified, to be kept sound and blameless at the coming of your Son. But I seem to have so many problems.

The one who calls you is faithful, and he will do this.

That may be the case, Lord, but all I can see are the times I fail to follow you—the times when I lose my temper with my spouse, get impatient with my children, or resent a coworker. It's so tempting to throw up my hands and give up any hope of ever being worthy of union with you.

The one who calls you is faithful, and he will do this.

But what about the limitations of my circumstances? I never seem to have the time to give you. So many days, I feel overwhelmed with the tasks that lie ahead of me. The burden that I'm carrying can feel so heavy at times that I can't imagine taking on anything else.

The one who calls you is faithful, and he will do this.

Yet I know you love me, and so I will take one step toward you and thank you that you truly are faithful. I will place a little faith in the fact that as constant as your calling is, your grace and power are constantly flowing out for me as well. Father, I trust that there is never a moment when you forget my needs.

The one who calls you is faithful, and he will do this.

Father, I believe you are faithful! I will turn to you now, and will continue to turn to you, so that you can fill up what is lacking in my resolve, my strength, my fortitude. I believe that as I turn to you, you will respond!

The one who calls you is faithful, and he will do this.

I rejoice in you, my Lord! I know that you don't call me to an impossible goal. You freely give what I need to reach the goal. The closer I get, the more intimately I know you, the easier it is to respond to you! Help me, Lord, as I take each step toward you. I want to gaze into your eyes as you call me to yourself, and know that indeed you are faithful and will accomplish it!

2 Thessalonians 1:1-5

1 Paul, Silvanus, and Timothy,
To the church of the Thessalonians in God our Father and the
Lord Jesus Christ:
2 Grace to you and peace from God our Father and the Lord
Jesus Christ.
3 We must always give thanks to God for you, brothers and sisters, as is right, because your faith is growing abundantly, and the
love of everyone of you for one another is increasing. 4 Therefore
we ourselves boast of you among the churches of God for your
steadfastness and faith during all your persecutions and the afflictions that you are enduring.
5 This is evidence of the righteous judgment of God, and is
intended to make you worthy of the kingdom of God, for which
you are also suffering.

This letter expresses thanksgiving to God for the Thessalonians—perhaps the most praised congregation of all the New Testament churches. Following in the footsteps of Paul (Acts 17:1-9), the Thessalonian Christians upheld their faith in the face of considerable hostility and persecution from their neighbors. The example of the Thessalonians was a light to other churches, for they witnessed to more than perseverance; they witnessed to a powerful work of God in their lives (2 Thessalonians 1:3-4).

The persecution which the Thessalonians faced was real: The Jews with whom they worshipped opposed their belief in Jesus as Messiah. As Christians began to form closely knit communities with other

Christians, society also began to look upon them with increasing suspicion. They did not bring suffering upon themselves through irresponsible behavior. Persecution was brought on by people opposed to them and their witness. But God used even this to strengthen the Thessalonians for the heavenly life to come.

The Thessalonians did not see persecution as something just to be endured; they knew that in all things God works his will (Romans 8:28). Their vision was focused upon the return of Jesus, when they would ultimately be repaid for the injustices they were enduring and be rewarded with the crown of life.

The witness of our parishes and churches today ought to be just as powerful as that of the Thessalonian church. Can people see the work of God among us when we worship? When we evangelize? When we serve? Can they see changes in us and in our fellow parishioners? They should be able to, for Christ Jesus is every bit as alive today as he was in the first century.

From the prayer for the Thessalonians (2 Thessalonians 1:11-12), we can gain light on how to pray for our own churches, that God may count us worthy of his calling. This is a calling no one ever earns, but it's a privilege God wants us to treasure by following him earnestly. We too can pray that God would bring to "mighty fulfillment" those acts or good purposes that are inspired by our faith. Inspired actions glorify the name of Jesus in this present age, and we will be glorified in Jesus when he returns to reign.

"Lord, we pray that our local churches can be beacons of light in our communities. May your church be a faithful bride and always be a cause for your name to be honored."

2 Thessalonians 1:6-12

6 For it is indeed just of God to repay with affliction those who
afflict you, 7 and to give relief to the afflicted as well as to us, when
the Lord Jesus is revealed from heaven with his mighty angels 8 in
flaming fire, inflicting vengeance on those who do not know God
and on those who do not obey the gospel of our Lord Jesus. 9 These
will suffer the punishment of eternal destruction, separated from
the presence of the Lord and from the glory of his might, 10 when
he comes to be glorified by his saints and to be marveled at on that
day among all who have believed, because our testimony to you
was believed. 11 To this end we always pray for you, asking that our
God will make you worthy of his call and will fulfill by his power
every good resolve and work of faith, 12 so that the name of our
Lord Jesus may be glorified in you, and you in him, according to the
grace of our God and the Lord Jesus Christ.

Imagine a traveler standing at a crossroads, staring at signs pointing in opposite directions. Like countless times before on his journey, he must choose which path he will take. If he has chosen the right direction each time, you wouldn't expect him to be overly surprised when he finally arrives at his chosen destination, would you?

We might flinch when we read of the final judgment, as Paul writes that "the Lord Jesus [will be] revealed from heaven with his mighty angels in flaming fire, inflicting vengeance on those who do not . . . obey the gospel of our Lord Jesus" (2 Thessalonians 1:7-8). But the final judgment of Jesus should come as no surprise, since it reflects decisions we have made throughout our lives. To be "separated from the presence of the Lord" (1:9) is the natural consequence in eternity of lifelong choices—big or small—to reject the gospel.

This passage is a rather direct invitation to let Jesus' word pierce our hearts and expose our sin. Do we seek God's power to overcome our weaknesses? Do we welcome, or turn away from, the spiritually or physically needy? Do we give of our time or talents to help others? As the *Catechism of the Catholic Church* teaches, "Our attitude about our neighbor will disclose acceptance or refusal of grace and divine love" (678).

St. Paul acknowledged that his primary responsibility was to pray for his flock, that God would "fulfill by his power every good resolve and work of faith" (2 Thessalonians 1:11). Paul was praying that every day the Thessalonians would respond to Christ and say "yes" to every impulse from the Holy Spirit! Similarly, St. Augustine warns the teacher of God's word: "If he is to obtain a good result, it will be due more to the piety of his prayers than to his gifts of speech" (*Christian Instruction*, 4,15).

How important it is for us to intercede for others! As we pray for the salvation of unbelievers and the faithfulness of believers, we see Jesus glorified and revealed in us here and now—a foretaste of the day when he comes "to be glorified by his saints and to be marveled at . . . among all who have believed" (2 Thessalonions 1:10).

"Lord Jesus, we lift up to you all the people we know. Come and strengthen those who believe, that they may continue on the road to holiness and eternal salvation. For those who have rejected you, may their hearts be turned so that they may finally be reconciled and reunited with you in heaven!"

2 Thessalonians 2:1-12

1 As to the coming of our Lord Jesus Christ and our being gathered
together to him, we beg you, brothers and sisters, 2 not to be quickly
shaken in mind or alarmed, either by spirit or by word or by letter, as
though from us, to the effect that the day of the Lord is already here.
3 Let no one deceive you in any way; for that day will not come
unless the rebellion comes first and the lawless one is revealed, the
one destined for destruction. 4 He opposes and exalts himself above
every so-called god or object of worship, so that he takes his seat in
the temple of God, declaring himself to be God. 5 Do you not
remember that I told you these things when I was still with you?
6 And you know what is now restraining him, so that he may be
revealed when his time comes. 7 For the mystery of lawlessness is
already at work, but only until the one who now restrains it is
removed. 8 And then the lawless one will be revealed, whom the
Lord Jesus will destroy with the breath of his mouth, annihilating
him by the manifestation of his coming. 9 The coming of the lawless
one is apparent in the working of Satan, who uses all power, signs,
lying wonders, 10 and every kind of wicked deception for those who
are perishing, because they refused to love the truth and so be saved.
11 For this reason God sends them a powerful delusion, leading them
to believe what is false, 12 so that all who have not believed the
truth but took pleasure in unrighteousness will be condemned.

"The end of the world is at hand!" People seem to be terrified by, and yet drawn to, descriptions of the end times. Admittedly, there is something in us that is excited by apocalyptic language. It's as if we feel the challenge to try to unravel its mysterious predictions and then see if we "got it right." But what is the purpose of the writer—in this case St. Paul—in using such language?

The *Catechism of the Catholic Church* sheds some light on Paul's words:

> The persecution that accompanies [the Church's] pilgrimage on earth will unveil the "mystery of iniquity" in the form of a religious deception offering men an apparent solution to their problems at the price of apostasy from the truth. The supreme religious deception is that of the Antichrist . . . by which man glorifies himself in place of God and of his Messiah come in the flesh. (675)

The heart of the lawlessness that will come before Jesus' return is the exaltation of humankind above God himself. We should not be surprised, because Satan sows confusion and lies, drawing people away from the truths of the gospel.

So the final battle appears to be the struggle between truth and falsehood. We may think of this as an epic struggle set for the end of time, but it is actually a struggle that goes on every day of our lives. The truth can make us uncomfortable, especially when it challenges us or exposes our sin or weakness. Wouldn't it be easier if we didn't have to face it at all? Maybe we could handle our lives on our own, without the all-seeing eyes of God over us, without his unreasonable demands on our behavior. But this approach runs contrary to the truth of the gospel, which brings redemption and freedom from sin, freedom to live an abundant life as a child of God.

In his respect for our decisions, God permits us to reap the consequences of refusing the truth. But if we hold fast to the gospel, accepting the forgiveness Jesus offers and walking each day as a child of God, we will not be shaken. In fact, loving the truth and standing firm in our faith is the best way to dispel anxieties about the Second Coming!

"Jesus, I long to see you in your glory! I know that times of deception will come, but I love your truth and will hold fast by your grace. Come, Lord Jesus!"

2 Thessalonians 2:13-17

13 But we must always give thanks to God for you, brothers and
sisters beloved by the Lord, because God chose you as the first fruits
for salvation through sanctification by the Spirit and through belief
in the truth. 14 For this purpose he called you through our proclamation of the good news, so that you may obtain the glory of our
Lord Jesus Christ. 15 So then, brothers and sisters, stand firm and
hold fast to the traditions that you were taught by us, either by
word of mouth or by our letter.
16 Now may our Lord Jesus Christ himself and God our Father,
who loved us and through grace gave us eternal comfort and good
hope, 17 comfort your hearts and strengthen them in every good
work and word.

We must always give thanks to God for you, brothers and sisters.
(2 Thessalonians 2:13)

Probably more than in any other texts, these Letters to the Thessalonians show how the early church was filled with frequent, spontaneous prayers of thanksgiving to God for his fatherly kindness.

For the fifth time in these two brief letters, Paul gives thanks for the believers in Thessalonica and for God's work of grace in their hearts. It seems that the early Christians really did have a grateful heart—maybe even that they were looking for reasons to give thanks to God for his loving involvement in their lives.

Paul's attitude—indeed, the attitude of the whole early church—can move us to ask whether we give thanks to God in the midst of events of our day. How easy it can be to grumble when we come upon obstacles or difficulties. Perhaps the pastor's homily goes a little long. Maybe our supervisor gives us an extra assignment at the end of the day, or someone cuts us off in traffic on the way home. Maybe our neighbor's dog barks throughout the night, or we just can't seem to shake the head cold that's been bothering us for the past few days. The list can go on and on.

As an experiment, try taking on an attitude of gratitude today. When the pastor speaks, maybe you can thank God for sending someone willing to dedicate himself to serving you and the others in your parish. When you see your supervisor, give thanks that you have a job. You might even try to consider the neighbor's barking dog as a messenger calling you to a midnight prayer session for the needs of family or friends!

When we make the effort to turn grumbling into thanksgiving, we will see our hearts and minds transformed. Instead of assuming the worst, we can look for the best. We can begin acknowledging that God has his hand on our lives and that his providential care for us can take on many forms—even those we least expect. We will probably be surprised to find that every decision we make to thank God actually makes our hearts more and more truly thankful!

"Heavenly Father, you are intimately involved in my life. I thank you for all the ways I see you at work throughout each day. You are not far off—you are close at hand, and I trust that I will see your work more clearly as I give you thanks."

2 Thessalonians 3:1-5

1 Finally, brothers and sisters, pray for us, so that the word of the
Lord may spread rapidly and be glorified everywhere, just as it is
among you, 2 and that we may be rescued from wicked and evil people; for not all have faith. 3 But the Lord is faithful; he will
strengthen you and guard you from the evil one. 4 And we have confidence in the Lord concerning you, that you are doing and will go
on doing the things that we command. 5 May the Lord direct your
hearts to the love of God and to the steadfastness of Christ.

How could a cloistered nun who rarely left her native town and died before her twenty-fifth birthday be called a patroness of the missions? Thérèse of Lisieux knew the secret that Paul tells the Thessalonians: "Pray for us, so that the word of the Lord may spread rapidly and be glorified everywhere, just as it is among you" (2 Thessalonians 3:1).

Young Thérèse longed to spread the gospel. However, because she felt called to join the cloistered Carmelites, there was no way she could be sent out as a missionary. Instead, she prayed fervently for those who worked in the mission fields, encouraged missionaries in her letters, and gladly embraced suffering and humiliation as a means of intercession for the church.

Paul recognized that the work of evangelization goes beyond mere human skill and requires spiritual support through prayer. Even if we are never sent out on an evangelistic mission, we are still essential to the work of missionaries. Our prayers in support of those men and women who proclaim the gospel provide a very real foundation for their successes.

Not only that—as we live our lives in loving obedience to Jesus and his teachings, we are an example to everyone that we meet. Like Thérèse, we can do little things that fill our days with great love for Jesus. Like the Thessalonians, we can continue to follow the example of our forefathers in faith, and the light of Christ will shine through us.

We can follow Thérèse's example and respond to Paul's request in simple ways each day. Take the news you hear on the radio or television as a cue to pray for those far from home engaged in missionary work. Maybe you can add a moment to pray for missions at the end of your daily prayer time, or before you leave Mass. Ask the Holy Spirit what would work for you, but know that the important thing is to try to remember to pray!

"Jesus, spread your word throughout the world! By the power of the Holy Spirit, open the ears of those who will hear the gospel today so that they will respond to your word. Protect the missionaries who often place their lives in danger to reach your lost sheep. May the truth of your love cover the earth!"

2 Thessalonians 3:6-10

6 Now we command you, beloved, in the name of our Lord Jesus
Christ, to keep away from believers who are living in idleness and
not according to the tradition that they received from us. 7 For you
yourselves know how you ought to imitate us; we were not idle
when we were with you, 8 and we did not eat anyone's bread without paying for it; but with toil and labor we worked night and day,
so that we might not burden any of you. 9 This was not because we
do not have that right, but in order to give you an example to imitate. 10 For even when we were with you, we gave you this command: Anyone unwilling to work should not eat.

The Thessalonians expected Jesus to return any day. Some even thought that the Day of the Lord was upon them. This thinking, fueled perhaps by a letter falsely purporting to be from Paul (2 Thessalonians 2:2), led some Thessalonians to believe that they no longer needed to work. Instead, they were idle and subsisted on the generosity of others. Paul sternly condemned such indolence, declaring finally, "Anyone unwilling to work should not eat" (3:10).

While Paul was adamant about the necessity of work, he wasn't just encouraging the Thessalonians to keep busy. Yes, idleness undermined the community, but more importantly, it undermined a fundamental truth: We have all been created in the image and likeness of God (Genesis 1:26-27). Immediately after breathing life into the first man and woman, God gave them a job to do: "Be fruitful and multiply, and fill the earth and subdue it" (1:28). To work is to take up our God-given duty as his children and to honor "the Creator's gifts and the talents received from him" (*Catechism of the Catholic Church*, 2427).

Working hard is right and healthy. As we obey God's command to have dominion through work, we fulfill "the potential inscribed in[our] nature" by God, who created us (CCC, 2428). Yet our work is not merely a duty, but also a privilege. Each of us has been called to advance the kingdom of God through the work we do—whether that means caring for an elderly relative, changing diapers, managing a sales force, or bagging groceries.

In whatever task we perform, we can both fulfill our potential and bring the light of Christ into the world. When our work serves the common good, it can carry on the work of God and contribute to his eternal purposes. In an early encyclical, Pope John Paul II urged, "Let the Christian who listens to the word of the living God, uniting work with prayer, know the place that his work has not only in *earthly progress* but also in the *development of the Kingdom of God*, to which we are all called through the power of the Holy Spirit" (*On Human Work*, 27).

"Holy Spirit, empower me to bring Christ into the world through the example that I give and the work I do today."

2 Thessalonians 3:11-18

11 For we hear that some of you are living in idleness, mere busy-
bodies, not doing any work. 12 Now such persons we command and
exhort in the Lord Jesus Christ to do their work quietly and to earn
their own living. 13 Brothers and sisters, do not be weary in doing
what is right.

14 Take note of those who do not obey what we say in this letter;
have nothing to do with them, so that they may be ashamed. 15 Do
not regard them as enemies, but warn them as believers.
16 Now may the Lord of peace himself give you peace at all times
in all ways. The Lord be with all of you.
17 I, Paul, write this greeting with my own hand. This is the mark
in every letter of mine; it is the way I write. 18 The grace of our
Lord Jesus Christ be with all of you.

Does the word *perseverance* make you a little nervous? Perseverance implies that you will be facing some difficulty, most likely one that will last quite a while. Or, you will need perseverance because whatever goal you have will not come easily. In today's world, where nearly every whim can be gratified instantly, the virtue of perseverance seems to have lost much of its appeal.

St. Paul knew how inconsistent people can be and how difficult it is to persevere. But some of his final words to the Thessalonians encouraged them: "Do not be weary in doing what is right" (2 Thessalonians 3:13). Why was it so important for Paul to get across this message? After all, he had praised the Thessalonians for their response to the gospel, imitating his example, and holding firm even in the midst of persecution. They already had a great track record!

Paul knew that only when believers continue in faithfulness to Jesus will they experience the deep peace that he prays for in verse sixteen. Every time a Christian chooses to listen to the Holy Spirit and turn away from sin, or chooses to obey the words of Jesus even when they are inconvenient, or decides to persist in daily prayer, he or she sets down the deep roots of perseverance. And what gives deeper peace than knowing in our hearts that we are doing all we can to follow Jesus?

How do we keep this peace among believers? At times, we need to deal with others who refuse to follow the gospel. Paul recommends that they be corrected with a spirit of brotherly love, but also that they be avoided so as not to give bad example to other believers. The goal of fraternal correction is to help others to persevere in following Christ, not to "punish" them.

We should not be surprised by our weaknesses, but we should also be confident. We have the power of the Holy Spirit to help us persevere. Pope John Paul II once said: "Fidelity always has to undergo the real test, that of endurance. . . . It is easy to live consistent [with one's beliefs] for a day or a few days. . . . But only a consistency which lasts right through life deserves the name 'fidelity'" (*Address in Mexico City Cathedral*, January 26, 1979).

"Lord Jesus, you persevered to the end. Give me the grace of perseverance, so that I may follow you no matter what, and rejoice at your coming at the end of my days."

Other Resources From The Word Among Us Press

The New Testament Devotional Commentary Series:

Matthew: A Devotional Commentary
Mark: A Devotional Commentary
Luke: A Devotional Commentary
John: A Devotional Commentary
Leo Zanchettin, General Editor

Enjoy praying through the gospels with commentaries that include each passage of Scripture with a faith-filled meditation.

The Wisdom Series:

Love Songs: Wisdom from Saint Bernard of Clairvaux
Live Jesus! Wisdom from Saints Francis de Sales and Jane de Chantal
A Radical Love: Wisdom from Dorothy Day
My Heart Speaks: Wisdom from Pope John XXIII
Welcoming the New Millennium: Wisdom from Pope John II
Touching the Risen Christ: Wisdom from The Fathers
Walking with the Father: Wisdom from Brother Lawrence
Hold Fast to God: Wisdom from The Early Church

These popular books include short biographies of the authors and selections from their writings grouped around themes such as prayer, forgiveness, and mercy.

Books on Saints:

A Great Cloud of Witnesses: The Stories of 16 Saints and Christian Heroes by Leo Zanchettin and Patricia Mitchell

I Have Called you by Name: The Stories of 16 Saints and Christian Heroes by Patricia Mitchell

Other Popular Resources:

God Alone: Stories of the Power of Faith
Twenty-eight real life stories that celebrate God's unconditional love.

Signposts: How To Be a Catholic Man in the World Today
By Bill Bawden and Tim Sullivan
Fifty-two discussion plans offer men the opportunity to grow in their faith.

To Order call 1-800-775-9673
or order online at www.wau.org